ARCHITECTURAL GUIDE BASEL 1980–2004

LUTZ WINDHÖFEL

ARCHITECTURAL GUIDE BASEL 1980–2004

A GUIDE THROUGH THE TRINATIONAL CITY

Birkhäuser – Publishers for Architecture
Basel · Boston · Berlin

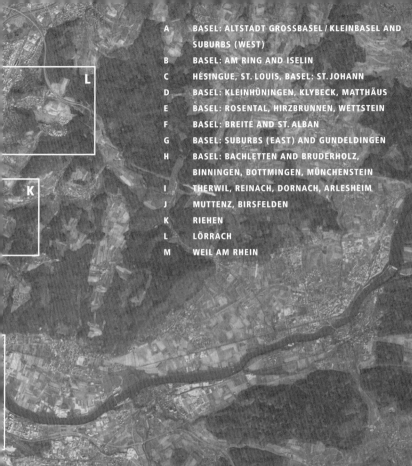

A	BASEL: ALTSTADT GROSSBASEL / KLEINBASEL AND SUBURBS (WEST)
B	BASEL: AM RING AND ISELIN
C	HÉSINGUE, ST. LOUIS, BASEL: ST. JOHANN
D	BASEL: KLEINHÜNINGEN, KLYBECK, MATTHÄUS
E	BASEL: ROSENTAL, HIRZBRUNNEN, WETTSTEIN
F	BASEL: BREITE AND ST. ALBAN
G	BASEL: SUBURBS (EAST) AND GUNDELDINGEN
H	BASEL: BACHLETTEN AND BRUDERHOLZ, BINNINGEN, BOTTMINGEN, MÜNCHENSTEIN
I	THERWIL, REINACH, DORNACH, ARLESHEIM
J	MUTTENZ, BIRSFELDEN
K	RIEHEN
L	LÖRRACH
M	WEIL AM RHEIN

CONTENTS

Foreword to the second, expanded edition

**Introduction: In Praise of Quality. New Developments in Architecture in and around Basel
Organization and Use**

A Basel: Altstadt Grossbasel / Kleinbasel and suburbs (West)

1   Morger & Degelo: Museum of Music, 1997–1999, Im Lohnhof 9

2   Gmür / Vacchini: Retail Building Conversion (Papyrus), 1999, Freie Strasse 43

3   Fierz & Baader: Conversion of Employment Office, 1983/1984, Utengasse 36

4   Silvia Gmür and Vischer AG: University Institute in the Engelhof, 1986–1990, Nadelberg 4

5   Fierz Architekten: University Administration Building, 2001–2003, Petersplatz 1

6   Naef, Studer & Studer: University Institute in the Rosshof (Economy Sciences Centre), 1984–1988, Petersgraben 49/51

7   Marbach & Rüegg: Residential and Office Building, 1984–1985, Spalenvorstadt 11

8   Herzog & de Meuron: Courtyard Residential Building, 1987–1988, Hebelstrasse 11

9   Herzog & de Meuron: Rossetti Building, Cantonal Hospital, 1997–1999, Spitalstrasse 26

10 Gmür / Vacchini: Klinikum 1, Cantonal Hospital Renovation, 1989–2003, Spitalstrasse 21

11 Gmür / Vacchini: Women's Clinic with Operating Theatres, 2000–2003, Spitalstrasse 21

B Basel: Am Ring and Iselin

12 Diener & Diener: Vogesen School, 1992–1996, St. Johanns-Ring 17 / Spitalstrasse

13 Fierz & Baader: Institute of Anatomy, University of Basel, 1993–1996, Pestalozzistrasse 20

14 Andrea Roost: Bio-Pharmazentrum of the University, 1996–2000, Klingelbergstrasse 50–70

15 Fierz & Baader: Training Workshop, 1992/1993, Missionsstrasse 47

16 Urs Gramelsbacher: Residential Building with Meeting Hall, 1993–1995, Missionsstrasse 37

17 Atelier-Gemeinschaft (Michael Alder, Hanspeter Müller, Roland Naegelin): Home for the Mentally Handicapped, 1997, Birmannsgasse 37

18 Brogli & Müller: Lindenhof Nursing Home, 1988–1991, Socinstrasse 30 / Eulerstrasse

19 Barcelo Baumann Architekten: Pavilion in Schützenmattpark, 2002–2003, Schützenmattpark 1

20 Alioth Langlotz Stalder Buol with Diener & Diener: "Holbeinhof" Seniors Residence and Nursing Home, 2000–2002, Leimenstrasse 67

21 Wilfrid and Katharina Steib: Public Prosecutor's Office and Municipal Jail, 1991–1995, Binningerstrasse 21 / Innere Margarethenstrasse 18

22 Richard Meier: Euregio Office Building, 1995–1998, Viaduktstrasse 40–44

23 Herzog & de Meuron: Residential and Office Building (formerly Schwitter), 1987–1988, Allschwilerstrasse 90 / Sierenzerstrasse / Colmarerstrasse

24 Peter Zinkernagel: Wasgenring Schoolhouse Expansion, 1994–1995, Blotzheimerstrasse 82

CONTENTS

C   Hésingue, St. Louis, Basel: St. Johann

25 Berrel Architekten: Single-Family House, Hésingue, 1996–1997, 42, rue de St. Louis

26 Daniel Stefani & Bernard Wendling: Kindergarten and Club House, St. Louis, 1992–1993, rue Anne de Gohr / rue de A. Baerenfels

27 Herzog & de Meuron: Pfaffenholz Sports Complex, St. Louis, 1992–1993, 5, rue de St. Exupéry

28 Herzog & de Meuron: REHAB – Swiss Centre for Paraplegics, Basel, 1999–2002, Im Burgfelderhof 40

29 Michael Alder: Luzernerring Housing Development, Basel, 1991–1993, Bungestrasse 10–28

30 Erny, Gramelsbacher, Schneider: Im Davidsboden Housing Development, Basel, 1989–1991, Gasstrasse / Vogesenstrasse

31 Miller & Maranta: Volta School, Basel, 1999–2000, Wasserstrasse 40 / Mülhauserstrasse

D   Basel: Kleinhüningen, Klybeck, Matthäus

32 Stefan Baader: IWB Central Storage, 1998–1999, Neuhausstrasse 31

33 Wilfrid and Katharina Steib: Wiesengarten Housing Development, 1983–1986, Wiesendamm / Altrheinweg / Giessliweg

34 Ackermann & Friedli: Ackermätteli School, 1995–1996, Rastatterstrasse 32

35 Morger & Degelo: Dreirosen School Expansion, 1990–1996, Breisacherstrasse 134 / Klybeckstrasse 111–115

36 Wilfrid and Katharina Steib: Marienhaus Nursing Home, 1993–1996, Horburgstrasse 54 / Markgräflerstrasse 47 / 49

37 Morger & Degelo: Housing Co-op, 1990–1993, Müllheimerstrasse 138 / 140

38 Diener & Diener: Hammer 1 Housing Development, 1978–1981, Hammerstrasse / Bläsiring / Efringerstrasse

39 Diener & Diener: Hammer 2 Housing Development, 1980–1985, Efringerstrasse / Amerbachstrasse / Riehenring

40 Wilfrid and Katharina Steib: Residential Building on the Water's Edge, 1994–1996, Unterer Rheinweg 48–52

E   Basel: Rosental, Hirzbrunnen, Wettstein

41 Morger & Degelo AG with Marques AG: High-rise for Basel Fair, 2000–2003, Messeplatz

42 Theo Hotz: New Fair Hall, 1998–1999, Messeplatz 1 / Riehenring / Isteinerstrasse

43 Diener & Diener: Studio Homes, Apartment Building and Hotel, 2000–2002, Isteinerstrasse 90–96, Schönaustrasse 10 and 31–35

44 Proplaning: Housing Development, 1997–1999, Schönaustrasse / Erlenstrasse

45 Christian Dill: Housing and Therapy Facility, 1992–1997, Riehenstrasse 300

46 Diener & Diener: Eglisee Supermarket (Migros), 1996–1997, Riehenstrasse 315

47 Michael Alder: Rankhof Stadium, 1993–1995, Grenzacherstrasse 351

48 Mario Botta: Jean Tinguely Museum, 1994–1996, Grenzacherstrasse 210

49 Diener & Diener: Warteckhof Development (former Warteck Brewery), 1994–1996, Grenzacherstrasse 62 / 64 / Fischerweg 6–10 / Alemannengasse 33–37

CONTENTS

F Basel: Breite and St. Alban

50 Scheiwiller & Oppliger: Breite Bathing Station on the Rhine, 1990 and 1993–1994, St. Alban-Rheinweg 195

51 Herzog & de Meuron: Central Switch-Yard, 1998–1999, Münchensteinerstrasse 115

52 Bürgin & Nissen in collaboration with Zwimpfer Partner: Swisscom (former Communications Centre), 1984–1989, Grosspeterstrasse 18

53 Herzog & de Meuron: St. Jakob Park, 1998–2002, St. Jakobs-Strasse 395

54 Proplaning: Sport-Toto Conversion, 1997, Lange Gasse 20

55 Burckhardt + Partner AG: Office Building, 1998–2000, Lange Gasse 15

56 Herzog & de Meuron: SUVA House (Swiss Accident Insurance), 1991–1993, St. Jakobs-Strasse 24 / Gartenstrasse 53/55

57 Mario Botta: BIS Administration Building (Bank for International Settlements, formerly UBS), 1990–1995, Aeschenplatz 1

G Basel: Suburbs (East) and Gundeldingen

58 Bürgin Nissen Wentzlaff: PAX Insurance Administration Building, 1992–1994 and 1995–1997, Aeschenplatz 13

59 Diener & Diener: Picassoplatz Businesscenter (former office building for Basel Life), 1990–1994, Lautengartenstrasse 6 / Dufourstrasse

60 Michael Alder: Conversion of Industrial Architecture, 1986, St. Alban-Tal 42

61 Urs Gramelsbacher: Residential Building, 1997–1999, St. Alban-Tal 38a

62 Diener & Diener: Residential Building with Craft Studios, 1984–1986, St. Alban-Rheinweg 94/96

63 Wilfrid and Katharina Steib: Museum of Contemporary Art, 1977–1980, St. Alban-Rheinweg 60

64 Schwarz-Gutmann-Pfister: New Schauspielhaus, 1999–2002, Steinentorstrasse 7

65 Diener & Diener: Residential Building with Office and Retail Space, 1994–1995, Steinenvorstadt 2 / Kohlenberg 1

66 Burckhardt + Partner AG: Leonhard High School, 1995–1998, Leonhardsstrasse 15

67 Cruz / Ortiz with Giraudi & Wettstein: Pedestrian Overpass at SBB Train Station, 2001–2003, Centralbahnplatz / Güterstrasse

68 Zwimpfer Partner: peter merian house, 1994–2000, Peter Merian-Strasse 80–90 / Nauenstrasse

69 Burckhardt + Partner AG: Office and Housing Complex, Thiersteinerallee, 2001–2003, Thiersteinerallee 14–30, Tellstrasse 48–52, 60–66

70 Diener & Diener: UBS Training and Conference Centre (formerly Swiss Bank Association), 1990–1994, Viaduktstrasse 33

H Basel: Bachletten and Bruderholz, Binningen, Bottmingen, Münchenstein

71 Wymann & Selva: Kaltbrunnen Schoolhouse, Basel, 1995–1996, Kaltbrunnenpromenade 95

72 Hanspeter Müller: Youth Centre, Binningen, 1995, In den Schutzmatten 10

73 Peter Stiner and August Künzel: Etoscha House in the Zoological Gardens, Basel, 1998–2003, Binningerstrasse 40

74 Silvia Gmür: One-Room House, Basel, 1990, Sonnenbergstrasse 92

75 Herzog & de Meuron: Exhibition Warehouse of the Laurenz Foundation, Münchenstein, 2000–2003, Ruchfeldstrasse 19

76 Berrel Architekten with Zwimpfer Partner Krarup Furrer: St. JakobArena, Münchenstein, 2001–2002, Brüglingen 33

77 Herzog & de Meuron: Plywood House, Bottmingen, 1985, Rappenbodenweg 6

78 Michael Alder: Single-Family House, Bottmingen, 1988, Kirschbaumweg 27

79 Ackermann & Friedli: Am Birsig Community Centre and Housing, Bottmingen, 1998–1999, Löchlimattstrasse 6

I Therwil, Reinach, Dornach, Arlesheim

80 Herzog & de Meuron: House for an Art Collector, Therwil, 1986, Lerchenrainstrasse 5

81 Morger & Degelo: Community Centre Reinach, 1998–2002, Hauptstrasse 10

82 Morger & Degelo: Single-Family House, Dornach, 1995–1996, Lehmenweg 2/Schlossweg

83 Proplaning: Obere Widen Residential Development, Arlesheim, 1997–1999, Birseckstrasse/Talstrasse

84 Klaus Schuldt and Andreas Scheiwiller: Zum wisse Segel, Villas, Arlesheim, 1997–2000, Zum wisse Segel 5, 7, 10, 11, 12

J Muttenz, Birsfelden

85 François Fasnacht: Office Building with Penthouse Apartment (Balimpex), Muttenz, 1995–1996, Frohburgerstrasse 21

86 Bürgin Nissen Wentzlaff: Hotel, Supermarket (Coop), Apartments, Muttenz, 1996–1998, St. Jakobs-Strasse 1/Hauptstrasse

87 Frank O. Gehry: Vitra-Center, Birsfelden, 1992–1994, Klünenfeldstrasse 22

88 Bürgin Nissen Wentzlaff: Bank and Office Building (Baselland Cantonal Bank), Birsfelden, 1994–1996, Hauptstrasse 75/77

K Riehen

89 Rolf Brüderlin: Hebel School Expansion, 1993–1994, Langenlängeweg 14

90 Metron Architekten: Im Niederholzboden Housing Development, 1992–1994, Im Niederholzboden/ Arnikastrasse 12–26

91 Rolf Furrer and François Fasnacht: Riehen Dorf Tram Shelter, 1995, Baselstrasse, and Lachenweg Bus Shelter, 1992, Lachenweg/Grenzacherweg

92 Stump & Schibli Architekten: "Zur Hoffnung" – Residential School for Children, 2000–2004, Wenkenstrasse 33

93 Renzo Piano: Beyeler Foundation Museum, 1994–1997 and 2000, Baselstrasse 101

94 Wilfrid and Katharina Steib: Haus zum Wendelin Nursing Home, 1986–1988, Inzlingerstrasse 50

95 Michael Alder: Vogelbach Housing Development, 1991–1992, Friedhofweg 30–80

L Lörrach

96 Günter Pfeifer: Single-Family House, 1992, Säckinger Strasse 26

97 Günter Pfeifer: Department Store Conversion into Library, 1992–1993, Baslerstrasse 128

98 Schaudt Architekten: Alt Stazione Cinema Café (house Zum Storchen), 1993–1996, Baslerstrasse 164/166

99 Detlef Würkert and Hans Ueli Felchlin: Housing Development, 1995–1998, Hangstrasse/Rebmannsweg

100 Wilhelm + Partner: Stadion Housing Development, 1990–1994, Haagenerstrasse / Wintersbuckstrasse

101 Detlef Würkert and Hans Ueli Felchlin: Nansenpark Housing Development, 1994–1997, Nansenstrasse 5 / 7 / Gretherstrasse / Haagenerstrasse

102 Wilfrid and Katharina Steib: Auf dem Burghof Theatre and Convention Complex, 1996–1998, Herrenstrasse 5

M Weil am Rhein

103 Nicholas Grimshaw: Vitra Furniture Factory, 1981, Charles-Eames-Strasse 2

104 Frank O. Gehry: Vitra Design Museum, 1988–1989, Charles-Eames-Strasse 1

105 Tadao Ando: Vitra Conference Pavilion, 1992–1993, Charles-Eames-Strasse 1

106 Alvaro Siza da Vieira: Vitrashop Factory Hall, 1992–1993, Charles-Eames-Strasse 2

107 Herzog & de Meuron: Frei Photo Studio, 1981–1982, Riedlistrasse 41

108 Zaha M. Hadid: Trinational Environmental Centre (previously Baden Württemberg Pavilion at National Garden Show «Grün 99»), 1996–1999, Mattrain 1

Illustration Index of Projects and Maps

Index of Names

Index of Building Types and Uses

FOREWORD TO THE SECOND, EXPANDED EDITION

The second edition of this guide, of which the German and English first editions from 2000 are out of print, contains sixteen new buildings and structures, which were completed at the beginning of this millennium. A total of nine projects from the first edition had to be dropped from this edition in order to present an updated guide to 108 buildings from a period of 24 years. Although difficult, this decision reflects the order of the day and is also intended as a homage to the readers.

The Olympic Stadium in Beijing for the 2008 Games, which is being erected according to plans by Herzog & de Meuron, has also brought international attention to the "St. Jakob Park" in Basel designed by the same architects (project 53/2002). The fair tower by Morger, Degelo and Marques (project 41/2003) is now the tallest building in Switzerland. The pedestrian overpass in the SBB railway station by Cruz/Ortiz and Giraudi & Wettstein (project 67/2003) shares the spotlight as the most important public structure with the University women's clinic by Gmür/Vacchini (project 11/2003). In the social sector, the Holbeinhof (project 20/2002), by architects Alioth, Langlotz, Stalder, Buol in collaboration with Diener & Diener, the therapeutic centre for paraplegics by Herzog & de Meuron (project 28/2002) and a residential school for children with disabilities by Stump & Schibli (project 92/2004) represent landmark contributions.

The cultural life of the city has gained new architectures in the theatre by Schwarz-Gutmann-Pfister (project 64/2002), the public warehouse of the Laurenz Foundation by Herzog & de Meuron (project 75/2003) and the pavilion in the Schützenmattpark by Barcelo Baumann (project 19/2003). Diener & Diener (project 43/2002) and Burckhardt + Partner (project 69/2003) created new housing and office spaces. With the Etoscha House, by Stiner and August Künzel (project 73/2003), the Zoological Gardens are featured in this architectural guide for the first time. The St. JakobArena by Berrel Architekten in collaboration with Zwimpfer Partner Krarup Furrer (project 76/2002) is a precious piece of the jigsaw in the city's largest sports complex. The new community centre in Reinach by Morger & Degelo (project 81/2002) and the careful restoration of the university administration building by Fierz Architekten (project 5/[1939]2003) underscore the importance of confident public buildings.

This guide, like its first edition, is based on a morphological-peripatetic reading of the city rather than on a political, geographic one. All projects presented in this guide can be reached on foot from the city centre (Basel Cathedral) without ever having to leave the world of densely developed streets.

L.W., March 2004

INTRODUCTION (TO THE FIRST EDITION, 2000)

IN PRAISE OF QUALITY

New Developments in Architecture in and around Basel

It is always difficult to determine the point at which the architecture of a city or a region comes of age, so to speak, and produces buildings of note. During the early years of functionalism in modern architecture, the 1920s and early 1930s, major developments in Berlin, Frankfurt am Main, Breslau (now Wroclaw), and Stuttgart were political and cultural showcase projects. For Basel, situated at the centre of the trinational area on the Upper Rhine, two projects in particular inspired a new way of looking at contemporary architecture: the Museum of Contemporary Art by Wilfrid and Katharina Steib (1977–1980) and the Hammer 1 housing development by Diener & Diener (1978–1981).

The Museum of Contemporary Art was created by converting and expanding a paper mill in Basel's late-medieval core, the old industrial quarter. When the last paper mill closed in 1956, Basel had been a centre for paper manufacturing for over five hundred years; printing and publishing houses in Basel relied on the local industry, and it was a high-quality export as well. Had the plans for the Museum of Contemporary Art been drawn up for the same site fifteen years earlier, the most likely outcome would have been a new construction. In 1964, for example, participants in the competition for the new town theatre were allowed to include plans for the demolition of the Elisabethenkirche in their submissions: fortunately, it did not come to that. Built between 1857 and 1865, the Elisabethenkirche is now considered the most important neo-Gothic church in Switzerland and a significant marker in the nation's architectural history. By the late 1970s, the demolition craze of the post-war period had subsided; new objective approaches to urban development led to an interest in establishing a dialogue with the industrial architecture along the Rhine. It was at this time that the developers in the St. Alban Valley district began to think contextually, integrating history into their plans.

The Hammer 1 housing development, across the Rhine from the museum, is notable for similar reasons: the housing project, like the museum, takes both past and present traditions into account. The designs are quite different, however. Regardless of its self-confident structure, formal language, and sheer mass, Hammer 1 was never designed to stand out. Instead, it was created from the outset to serve the residents and the city. Hammer 1 was built on the site of a former factory. In the nineteenth century, the city grew rapidly in this area; most buildings are no more than 120 years old. The new housing development has brought an influx of young tenants, making Hammer 1 the object of a major urban sociology study. The complex proved equally popular with the public and the media, and in 1985 Diener & Diener was able to open the doors to its sister development across the street, Hammer 2. Together, these two developments continue to have an enormous positive impact on the Matthäus and Rosental quarters on the right bank of the Rhine.

The Museum of Contemporary Art has had a similar influence, although its immediate environment is characterized by structures that are over a thousand years old, many of them heritage buildings. The former industrial quarter – an adventure playground for children in the 1950s – underwent a complete renewal in the 1970s under the auspices of the Christoph Merian Foundation, when it was transformed into an attractive residential area. The few empty lots that were available served as sites for new buildings designed by Michael Alder, Diener & Diener, and Urs Gramelsbacher.

The architects were not the only ones responsible for the atmosphere of revitalization in Basel; members of the municipal public housing and planning department, developers, builders, consultants, and the building trades all contributed. Around 1980, when both the Museum of Contemporary Art and Hammer 1 were under construction, three people in particular held key positions. These were Carl Fingerhuth, state architect (1979–1993); Rolf Fehlbaum, an economist and sociologist, and CEO of Vitra (since 1977); and architect and author Werner Blaser (since 1980). The potential of these early designs – which created pairings of history and substance, the museum and the here-and-now, industry and housing, revitalization and urbanization – took on a dynamic sense of purpose under Fingerhuth, Fehlbaum, and Blaser.

As director of the department of public housing and planning, Fingerhuth administered an impressive annual construction budget (1999: 120 million Swiss francs, or US$ 75 million). During his tenure, the municipality worked closely with local architectural firms to create projects of international calibre. Fingerhuth promoted the improvement of architectural competitions in terms of both scope and quality. Private sector clients – individuals and enterprises alike – began to look towards the municipal authority for help in organizing serious competitions.

While Fingerhuth's main motivation was to serve the public interest, Rolf Fehlbaum's position as CEO of Vitra gave him a more entrepreneurial outlook. His firm has been producing furniture designed by Charles and Ray Eames since 1957, and there is a natural link between these products and knowledge of the office and home environments. Furniture often corresponds to the architecture in which it is housed. It can be architectonic in design; as products of a specific culture, furniture designs sometimes become classic icons of an era or style. When Fehlbaum decided to expand the Vitra complex located in the German town of Weil am Rhein just outside of Basel, he hired internationally renowned architects. This proved to be an inspiration to local architects, some of whom collaborated with the international firms. By 1981, Nicholas Grimshaw's new furniture factory for Vitra had opened its doors. The British architect created several other buildings for the company before turning the project over to his colleague Frank Gehry, who is based in California.

Werner Blaser's role is more difficult to define. He initiated the "Basel Lectures on Architecture" in 1980 and has been influential behind the scenes.

Blaser's list of speakers has thus far included major contemporary thinkers as well as architectural visionaries. Most architects of note have come to Basel on Blaser's invitation. Richard Meier's first building in Switzerland (the 1990–1998), to cite one example, was the result of Blaser introducing the architect to the builder. Blaser has mediated many other introductions and contacts of this kind.

The roles played by Fingerhuth, Blaser, and Fehlbaum in recent developments in the architecture of Basel have varied, but all three have been characterized by terms such as mediation and trust, listening and seeing, rejecting prejudice and welcoming internationalism, knowledge and intellect. When these qualities were combined with the solid potential already in evidence in the local building industry, the result was a closely knit web of planning and aesthetics, of sociology and history, of psychology and intellect, the synergism of which has created a vital architectural culture.

A further decisive step occurred with the 1984 opening of the Architecture Museum. Another milestone year was 1988; in that year, more projects that would change the architectural image of the city were built than in any preceding year. Herzog & de Meuron completed their office and residential building on Allschwilerstrasse, and Michael Alder, his single-family house in Bottmingen. Morger & Degelo expanded a multi-family building on Gundeldingerstrasse with minimal intervention to the existing fabric. Bürgin & Nissen, in cooperation with Zwimpfer Partner, completed the large telephone exchange building near Münchensteiner bridge. The Rosshof building by Naef, Studer & Studer altered the Petersgraben streetscape. A few hundred metres further on, Herzog & de Meuron finished their courtyard residential building, their most prestigious project at the time in addition to the Ricola warehouse in Laufen. Also in 1988, the Wendelin House nursing home designed by Wilfrid and Katharina Steib was opened. This level of architectural growth at the end of the 1980s remains unsurpassed.

Gradually the public became more aware of Fehlbaum's projects. The opening in 1989 of the Design Museum by Frank Gehry, his first building in Europe, was a media event. People began speaking of an expressionist triangle in France, Germany, and Switzerland, formed by Gehry's museum, Le Corbusier's Notre Dame du Haut in Ronchamp (1950–1954), and Rudolf Steiner's Goetheanum in Dornach (1928). These comparisons gained momentum with the expressionistic architecture of Zaha M. Hadid's Vitra fire station in 1993. With the Design Museum providing a stimulating space for exhibitions, the town of Weil am Rhein suddenly became an attractive destination for the culturally jaded citizens of Basel to the south. Moreover, the new museum in Weil and the Museum of Architecture in Basel have benefited from a mutual exchange.

The onset of the new architecture in Basel was marked by a fresh approach to history and to the city, which intensified at the end of the 1980s. It is generally agreed that the Münster and the houses on the cathedral square are sacrosanct heritage buildings, each hundreds of years old. Nevertheless, Wilfrid and Katharina Steib were permitted to convert a residential dwelling into a research institute for musicology (Paul Sacher Foundation, 1982–1985 and 1996–1998). And in the late-medieval core of the Old City (dating from after the earthquake in 1356), nearly forty houses were renovated for contemporary living. By far the most striking example was Santiago Calatrava's sensitive renovation of a prestigious medieval building for use by a small theatre company (1986–1988). The high point of this building in the historic city was the renovation and conversion of the Engelhof by Silvia Gmür and Vischer Architects (1986–1990). The earliest reference to the historic building appears in a document from 1347. The original structure grew into an impressive patrician palace, and in 1499 this is where the peace treaty between France, Germany, and Switzerland was signed. Today, the building houses the university departments of German and Slavic languages and literatures, as well as a two-storey library and all other facilities required for such an institution. The building epitomizes the dialogue between old and new that is the hallmark of Basel's contemporary architecture.

While Vitra caused a stir by bringing in international names, Basel's own architects drew international attention with significant projects abroad. First, Michael Alder and Diener & Diener built in Salzburg: Alder created a much discussed school complex (1989) and Diener & Diener, a residential development (1986–1989). The Pilotengasse development in Vienna by Herzog & de Meuron in collaboration with Adolf Krischanitz and Otto Steidle (1989–1992) was the first large-scale project of the Basel team outside of Switzerland. Alder went on to a project in Stuttgart (residential building, 1991/1992), but from the early 1990s onwards Herzog & de Meuron and Diener & Diener were the dominant firms in terms of major competition awards or direct commissions.

Herzog & de Meuron built in Munich (Sammlung Goetz, 1989–1992), in Dijon (student residence, 1990–1992), in California (Dominus Winery, 1995–1998), and in Eberswalde, Germany (library and university institute, 1994–1999). They won major competitions in Munich (Bayerische Hypotheken- und Wechselbank, 1994), in London (Tate Gallery of Modern Art, 1995), and most recently in San Francisco (De Young Museum, 1999). Diener & Diener, too, have focused on cultural projects: an exhibition pavilion in Cologne (Galerie Gmurzynska, 1990), the renovation of a museum in Berlin (Natural History Museum, since 1995), and a university building in Gothenburg (library and institutes, since 1997). In addition, they are internationally active in housing construction: Paris (1992–1996), Berlin (since 1994), and Amsterdam (since 1995). International competitions are always carefully monitored by the local architectural community, and the winners benefit from widespread media attention. The list of exhibitions devoted to the two Basel firms is equally impressive in Munich and Paris (Herzog & de Meuron) as it is in London, Berlin, Copenhagen, and Madrid (Diener & Diener). Other firms in the city occasionally enter the limelight. Ernst Spycher completed a much-admired high school in Freiburg, (1993–1997). In 1998 Morger & Degelo won the competition in Vaduz, Liechtenstein, for a new museum of art. And Berrel Architects built a single-family house (1996–1997) in the French quarter (Hésingue) that has set new standards in this category.

INTRODUCTION

Basel's tightly knit architectural culture developed its own dynamic at the beginning of the 1990s. Private and public clients together with the community of architects shared criteria for quality standards, which although they weren't defined or written down, nevertheless seemed to form a natural basis for the discussion on architecture. They categorically rejected designs that fell outside this architectural vocabulary. When Mario Botta won a competition in 1986 to design the local branch of a major Zurich bank, the Ticino architect's vision was met by a fierce polemic which subsided only gradually, even after the building was completed in 1995. However heated at times, the dialogue on architecture has had a positive impact that far outweighs any differences of opinion. Ultimately, the interaction between the architectural scene and the general public has increased the awareness of the importance of architecture in the cultural life of a city.

The publicity generated around buildings designed by international stars also benefited local architects, whose reputation quickly spread beyond the Swiss borders. In 1993 and 1994, for example, Tadao Ando, Alvaro Siza, Zaha M. Hadid, and Frank Gehry designed new buildings for Vitra. During the same period, the Swiss firms Herzog & de Meuron and Diener & Diener completed major projects: the former, a sports centre and a residential and office building; the latter, a large training centre. By 1995, when the Museum of Modern Art in New York included Herzog & de Meuron's competition model for the copper-clad railway signal tower in an exhibition, such international attention no longer seemed surprising.

Demographically, too, Basel's building boom occurred at an opportune time. There was a surge in the number of school-age children in the late 1980s and statistics indicated continued population growth for the years to come. These demographic factors coincided with school reforms, implemented in 1994. A unique intensification in school development was the direct result of this confluence of events. Existing facilities were renovated and expanded, some of them extensively, and new buildings were erected throughout the canton of Basel. Public recreational facilities and industrial buildings were converted into school buildings, resulting in idiosyncratic solutions.

These development strategies profiled the capabilities of the local architects and demonstrated their sensitive treatment of historic structures. For new school buildings the canton was generally able to offer generous, well-treed building sites, allowing for highly creative designs. The greatest number of projects, however, were concentrated in existing school facilities, often comprising several buildings from different eras, anywhere between forty to a hundred years old. Time and again, these conversion and expansion projects revealed the high quality of earlier architectural periods in the Upper Rhine region. As in other areas of urban development, the public building projects for the city's educational infrastructure contributed to a general awareness of architecture. And last but not least, the boom in school construction provided a much-needed financial boost to many of the younger firms in the city.

While commercial buildings commissioned by the business community created new urban accents, the greatest impact resulted from initiatives set in motion by leading figures in Basel's cultural establishment. Two in particular are notable in this context: the art collector and gallery owner Ernst Beyeler, and the conductor, music patron, and entrepreneur Paul Sacher. Beyeler had formed an impressive collection of modern classics in his fifty years as an art dealer; he commissioned Renzo Piano to build a museum for his private foundation (1992–1997 and 2000). Sacher founded a museum dedicated to his longtime friend, the sculptor Jean Tinguely. The building was designed and realized by Mario Botta (1993–1996) on the occasion of the hundredth anniversary of the firm of F. Hoffmann-La Roche. Both museums quickly became tourist attractions, to a large degree because of the buildings themselves, which inspire a keen interest in the architecture itself. Botta created an ideal environment for Tinguely's clamorous machines by designing an 1800-square-metre, column-free exhibition hall. Piano's museum, on the other hand, is distinguished by its sophisticated and delightful integration of space and materials, thus providing an appropriate home for the exquisite paintings and sculptures of the Beyeler Foundation. Moreover, each building benefits from a location in harmony with its architecture. Botta's museum is situated on the banks of the Rhine and, despite the close proximity to the inner city, the main facade overlooks a small park. Piano's building is located in a suburb next to a historic country estate and is situated on a hillside above a fluvial plain rich in animal life. Although it was completed only a few years ago, Piano's structure has already gained a world-class reputation and is generally regarded as one of the most famous exponents of the genre.

It is possible to walk from Renzo Piano's Beyeler Foundation Museum in Riehen to Frank Gehry's Vitra Design Museum in Weil am Rhein. One hardly notices the border to Germany, as customs officials check passports only sporadically. The same goes for the border crossing between Riehen and Lörrach, and the distance too is comparable to that between Riehen and Weil am Rhein, again easily covered on foot or by public transit. In Lörrach, visitors will encounter yet another building designed for cultural use whose architecture attracted immediate attention when it was completed. This is the new Burghof theatre, concert, and convention complex, a multifunctional cultural centre designed by Wilfrid and Katharina Steib (1995–1998). The complex offers facilities for any type of theatre and music performance, with an audience capacity of nearly a thousand people. The Burghof was publicly funded by the city of Lörrach, and reaction among the citizens has been mixed. The aesthetics of the unusual architecture and its impact on the urban landscape have sparked a certain amount of controversy. The municipal building authorities and leading figures in the local community defend and praise the project, but the general public is less inclined to appreciate it.

This triangle of extraordinary cultural buildings in the northern section of Basel and its trinational environs is truly a phenomenon, especially when we consider that no deliberate plan or coordination preceded it: Gehry built for a commercial enterprise; Piano, for a private foundation; Wilfrid and Katharina Steib, for a municipality. An aerial view reveals that the structures mark the coordinates of a nearly perfect isosceles triangle – serendipity, no doubt – yet one may be forgiven for attaching some symbolic value to it. Like the museums, the Burghof complex is a challenging and animating presence in its immediate environment. Gehry's building, already ten years old in 1999, is visited by a steady stream of architectural pilgrims. In Europe, Gehry's designs are gradually gaining a place in the canon of classic deconstructionism. The sculptural building with its 740 square metres of exhibition space is more compact and much more precise than Gehry's 1997 colossus for the Guggenheim Foundation in Bilbao with its 17 000 square metres of floor space. As for the Beyeler Foundation Museum, it is difficult to know whether the huge stream of visitors comes or the art or the architecture – most likely for both, in view of their inspired symbiosis. The number of visitors during the first twenty months (500 000) was so great that Piano added a 12-metre expansion to the north side of the building facing the German border, creating an additional space of 560 square metres distributed across two floors. By increasing the property to accommodate the addition, the architect was able to leave the landscaped park untouched, thus maintaining the delicate balance between architecture and designed nature that had been achieved in the original concept.

Riehen, a quiet, almost rural town (administered as part of the canton of Basel), was soon faced with a jolt to its pastoral atmosphere: the museum invited avant-garde artists Christo and Jeanne-Claude to stage "Wrapped Trees" for 1998. Estimates predicted that some 300 000 visitors would stream into the town over a period of a few weeks. Hence a multi-storey car park was urgently required.

INTRODUCTION

Wilfrid and Katharina Steib's Burghof complex in Lörrach is still too new to assess its attractiveness for visitors or its full impact on future development in this large district town in Baden-Württemberg, although the city has already flanked the building with several new designs and conversions. Thus a central department store building dating back to the turn of the last century was converted into a public library (Günter Pfeifer, 1992/1993). And the main street in the city core and the square in front of the Burghof were accentuated with large public sculptures (by Ulrich Rückriehm, Stephan Balkenol, and Bruce Nauman).

The most recent examples of good construction are almost all located in Basel itself, in the downtown core as well as on the periphery. Miller & Maranta built the new Volta schoolhouse near the Rhine (1999/2000). The massive rectangular tower of the Pharmazentrum (designed by Andrea Roost, 1996–2000) was added to the university's Biozentrum. Zwimpfer Partner created an office complex that resembles a glass shrine, the peter merian house (1994–2000), next to the Schweizer Bahnhof (railway station) and diagonally across from the new railway signal tower (Herzog & de Meuron, 1998/1999). Near Basel's main traffic intersection, the Aeschenplatz, Burckhardt Partner completed an exemplary office building (1998–2000), and, last but not least, the historic centre of the city saw the opening of the Lohnhof Museum of Music (Morger & Degelo, 1997–1999).

This book neither could nor is intended to rival Dorothee Huber's "Architekturführer Basel: Die Baugeschichte der Stadt und ihrer Umgebung" (1993). Huber treats the history from the first Celtic settlements to the beginning of the 1990s, a period of over 2000 years. The book at hand deals much more modestly with only the last twenty years.

ORGANIZATION AND USE

The projects presented in this architectural guide are distributed across three national borders and many local and regional areas. We have therefore organized the entries in accordance with existing administrative and planning entities. The interconnected urban area between Hésingue and St. Louis in the west (France), Dornach and Arlesheim in the south (Switzerland), Muttenz and Birsfelden in the east (Switzerland), and Lörrach and Weil am Rhein in the north (Germany) has been divided into thirteen urban districts, or chapters. Preceding each chapter is a map of the district, which locates the buildings for visitors.

The order of the chapters follows the borders of the local land registry offices in the case of the self-governing municipalities in France and Switzerland. The canton of Basel-Stadt was subdivided according to the official documents of the department of public housing and planning (Residential Neighbourhoods and Statistical Districts in Canton Basel-Stadt). Annexed communities and satellite districts as they exist in Lörrach were disregarded for the purposes of this book, since they are separate and some distance from the city proper.

The sequence from chapter to chapter and from project to project within each chapter approximates a route that reflects the geographic proximity between buildings in one and the same district while at the same time taking care to establish links between chapters. Neighbouring projects in adjacent districts are also marked in the map section preceding the relevant chapter; sometimes, they are also cross-referenced in the text.

This architectural guide can also be used in other ways, facilitated by means of two indices at the back: an index of names, which includes the names of architectural firms (e.g., Herzog & de Meuron) and an index of building types and uses (residential buildings, sports and recreational facilities, administrative and cultural buildings, etc.), a valuable tool for planners and architects.

ORGANIZATION AND USE

The region of Basel has an excellent public transportation system. In addition to parking zones, the maps that accompany each chapter indicate the relevant bus and tram lines and the stops closest to the various projects listed in the guide. This information – updated on May 2004 – is also contained in the general data given for each project beneath the address.

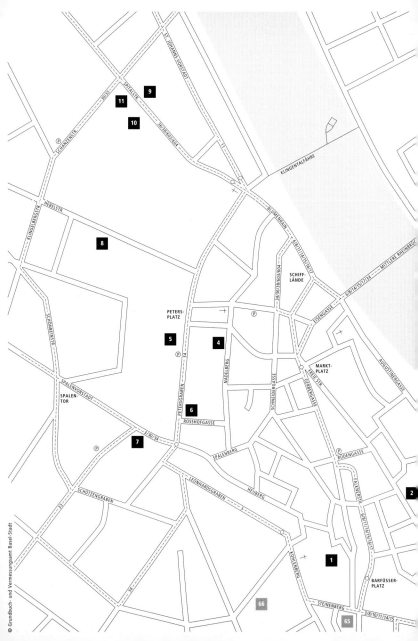

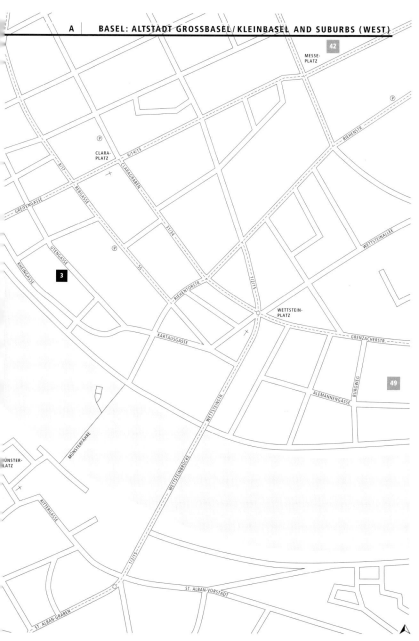

Architect:	Morger & Degelo, Spitalstrasse 8, 4056 Basel
Client:	Canton Basel-Stadt, Department of civil services
	and environment, Planning department, Münsterplatz 11, 4001 Basel
Dates:	project planning 1996, construction 1997–1999

MUSEUM OF MUSIC

Im Lohnhof 9, 4051 Basel | Tram 3: Musik-Akademie | Tram 3 6 8 11 14 15 16 17: Barfüsserplatz

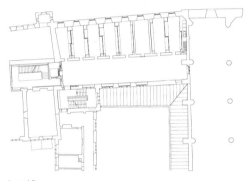

Second floor

The Lohnhof is a thousand-year-old complex, which Morger & Degelo have converted into a museum. Originally, the site was occupied by a church (founded in 1002) to which other sacred buildings were added over the years. After some time, these were used as a jail. As far back as the twelfth century, the complex was incorporated into medieval fortifications. The modern conversion has created apartments, a hotel restaurant, and cultural facilities. For the first time, there is space to exhibit the Museum of History's collection of musical instruments. Within strict preservation regulations, an exhibition space (600 m^2) across four storeys has been created in the former prison wing. The minimal, sparse atmosphere is an ideal environment for the exhibitions.

Entrance courtyard

Architect:	Gmür/Vacchini, Pfluggässlein 3, 4001 Basel
Client:	Papyrus AG, Freie Strasse 43, 4001 Basel
Dates:	project planning 1997, construction 1999

RETAIL BUILDING CONVERSION
Freie Strasse 43, 4001 Basel | Tram 3 6 8 11 14 15 16 17: Barfüsserplatz

Stairwell across four floors

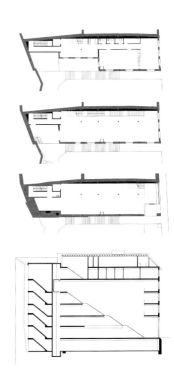

Sixth floor

Fourth floor

Ground floor

Longitudinal section

In recent years, monumental stairs have become an important motif in Basel's contemporary architecture: the most recent example is Silvia Gmür's and Livio Vacchini's design for a paper and art supply store on Freie Strasse. Narrow, single-file stairs connect four floors in a stairwell placed next to the building's right fire wall. Each landing leads to a different department, which are accentuated with muted but deep colours. From the street the added stairwell is visible only on the first two floors, which are fully glazed. This is a rigorous modernization of this narrow building, originally designed by Suter & Burckhardt in 1911.

Architect:	Fierz & Baader, Basel
	Since 1995 Fierz Architekten, Leimenstrasse 76, 4051 Basel
	and Stefan Baader, Güterstrasse 144, 4002 Basel
Client:	Canton Basel-Stadt, Department of civil services and environment,
	Planning department, Münsterplatz 11, 4001 Basel
Dates:	construction 1983–1984

CONVERSION OF EMPLOYMENT OFFICE

Utengasse 36, 4058 Basel | Tram 6 8 14 15 17, Bus 34: Rheingasse
Tram 1 2 15, Bus 31 34: Wettsteinplatz

Ground-floor hall

The cantonal employment office, a massive stone building, was designed by E. Heman in 1931/1932 in a conservative style, although it claimed kinship to a similar building designed by Walter Gropius in Dessau in the 1920s. With a few structural changes in the ground-floor layout, new large window surfaces, carefully chosen stone floors, and a contemporary lighting system, the recent conversion by Fierz & Baader has given the building a contemporary face. The original entrance on Rheingasse was too narrow; the new, more generously proportioned entrance lies on Utengasse, previously the rear of the building. The stone-faced columns resemble minimalist sculptures.

Facade on Utengasse

North-south section

Architect:	Silvia Gmür, Pfluggässlein 3, 4001 Basel
	Associate Christoph Butscher
	in collaboration with Vischer AG, Hardstrasse 10, 4006 Basel
Client:	Canton Basel-Stadt, Department of civil services and environment,
	Planning department, Münsterplatz 11, 4001 Basel
Dates:	construction 1986–1990

UNIVERSITY INSTITUTE IN THE ENGELHOF

Nadelberg 4, 4051 Basel | Tram 3, Bus 34: Universität | Tram 6 8 11 14 15 16 17: Marktplatz

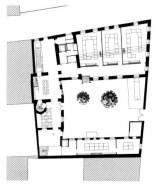

Ground floor

The history of the Engelhof goes back to the eleventh century. Its current shell dates mostly from the sixteenth century. The interior, however, has undergone a radical change in this conversion of the building into seminar facilities for the University of Basel. Metal stairs, fine carpentry in clean forms, and prototype lighting fixtures give the building a contemporary look. Perhaps no other conversion or modification in the building's long history has had a comparable impact: the result is a profound visual harmonization of the space. One would have to travel far to find another library that is as tranquil, focused, and absolutely contemporary. It occupies two floors beneath a gable roof.

Band of skylights in reading area

Two-storey library

Architect:	Fierz Architekten, Leimenstrasse 76, 4051 Basel
Client:	Canton Basel-Stadt, Department of civil services and environment,
	Planning department, Münsterplatz 11, 4001 Basel
Dates:	project planning 2000, construction 2001–2003

UNIVERSITY ADMINISTRATION BUILDING
Petersplatz 1, 4003 Basel | Tram 3, Bus 30 33: Spalentor | Bus 34: Universität

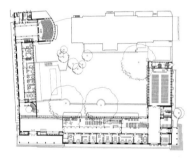

Ground floor plan

The main administration building of the University of Basel on the Petersplatz – designed by Roland Rohn and opened for occupation in 1939 – has been restored (lighting fixtures, furniture), renovated (windows, sanitary installations, building services) and converted (administrative area, basement level). Fierz Architekten have preserved the dignity of the important historic building, reinvigorated the bright interior and the imposing exterior. Half of the eighteen lecture halls were restored and modernized: most of the chairs by Häfeli, Moser, and Steiger were preserved. The glass front overlooking the garden runs parallel to the internal corridor in the north wing. The interior space (with the new café-restaurant) is now linked to the enclosed courtyard park at several points. An open-plan space with PC workstations was created in the basement level. A simplified, discrete lighting scheme once again allows the 70-metre-long ribbon of windows on the upper floor to come into full effect. The same is true for the elegant spiral staircase with skylight, which connects the U-shaped ensemble on the Petersgraben side.

Foyer with spiral staircase

A conference room on the upper floor

Architect:	Naef, Studer & Studer, Zürich
Client:	Canton Basel-Stadt, Department of civil services and environment,
	Planning department, Münsterplatz 11, 4001 Basel
Dates:	conceptual competition 1979, project competition 1980, construction 1984–1988

UNIVERSITY INSTITUTE IN THE ROSSHOF

Petersgraben 49/51, 4051 Basel | Tram 3, Bus 34: Universität | Tram 6 8 11 14 15 16 17: Marktplatz

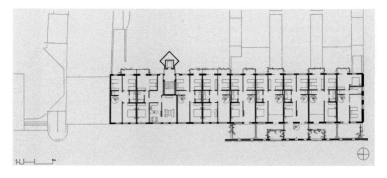

Fifth floor

The construction of the new Rosshof was a hot political topic for years and the very fact that it was finally realized makes it significant in terms of urban planning. Naef, Studer & Studer erected a complex cubature whose formal aesthetics and physicality are convincing. The new complex provides 5000 square metres of floor space for the university's Institute of Economics. The six-storey building on Petersgraben also contains sixteen apartments ranging from 2.5 to 5.5 rooms. Two shops as well as some 400 underground parking spaces round out the building program. In one corner of the lot, a wing that contains a lecture hall cleverly integrates an historic fifteenth-century building into the complex.

Courtyard with
historic building

Facade overlooking Petersgraben

Architect:	Ueli Marbach (Arcoop), Kappelerstrasse 16, 8001 Zürich
	in collaboration with Arthur Rüegg, Forchstrasse 37, 8008 Zürich
	Associate Cornelia Zürcher, site management Architeam 4 Basel
Client:	Canton Basel-Stadt, Department of civil services and environment,
	Planning department, Münsterplatz 11, 4001 Basel
Dates:	competition 1981, construction 1984–1985

RESIDENTIAL AND OFFICE BUILDING

Spalenvorstadt 11, 4051 Basel | Tram 3, Bus 34: Universität

Site plan with fourth-floor plan

Facade facing Spalenvorstadt

The terrace on the fourth floor

The residential and office building on Spalenvorstadt by architects Ueli Marbach and Arthur Rüegg fills a gap between nineteenth-century buildings. The entrance to the municipal fire station is located here: a 5-metre-wide and 4-metre-high portal, it is the most visible component of the building. A recessed balcony was placed above it along the same line. The square main room of the upstairs apartment receives light from a covered courtyard. Room-height glass-brick walls let daylight into the floors above. Two floors have large balconies on the courtyard side – all this in a central location!

Architect:	Herzog & de Meuron, Rheinschanze 6, 4056 Basel
	Project management Mario Meier
Client:	Canton Basel-Stadt, Department of civil services and environment,
	Planning department, Münsterplatz 11, 4001 Basel
Dates:	competition 1984, construction 1987–1988

COURTYARD RESIDENTIAL BUILDING

Hebelstrasse 11, 4056 Basel | Bus 30 33: Bernoullianum | Tram 3, Bus 34: Universität

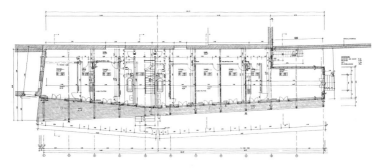

Ground floor

A small residential building, which lies parallel to a dividing wall in a courtyard on Hebelstrasse, has fascinated the public ever since it was first completed. The three-storey building with oak siding is raised on Japanese-style wooden supports. It contains six apartments in this quiet urban location. The project brought international attention to the architects. The verandahs are accessible from all the interiors in a sophisticated integration of interior and exterior space. The ground-floor verandah is reached via two steps. This building seems to float above the ground, reminiscent of sacred wooden architecture in the Far East. Bamboo in the gravel-covered yard reinforces this association.

Oak facade

Slim volume against wall

Architect:	Herzog & de Meuron, Rheinschanze 6, 4056 Basel
	Project management Mathis S. Tinner
Client:	Canton Basel-Stadt, Department of civil services and environment,
	Planning department, Münsterplatz 11, 4001 Basel
Dates:	project planning 1995, construction 1997–1999

ROSSETTI BUILDING, CANTONAL HOSPITAL

Spitalstrasse 26, 4056 Basel | Tram 11: Johanniterbrücke | Bus 30 33 36 38 603 604: Frauenspital

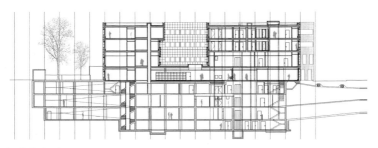

Longitudinal section

On a 7000-square-metre property surrounded by historic buildings from the last 270 years, Herzog & de Meuron erected the new Institute for Hospital Pharmaceutics. The four-storey building rises from an underground structure that dates back to the 1960s. The basic dimensions of the plan were thus predetermined. The facade design – glazing with a screen-printed pattern of bottle-green dots – was inspired by glass objects in the city's pharmaceutical museum. This has resulted in a 1500-square-metre glass sculpture on the edge of the city's downtown. At the main entrance, a section of the glass has been replaced by an ivy-covered honeycomb wall.

Facade on courtyard side

Facade on Spitalstrasse

Architect:	Gmür/Vacchini, Pfluggässlein 3, 4001 Basel; for Klinikum 1 Ost (East),
	in collaboration with Kurt Nussbaumer, Toffol+Berger, Suter+Suter (all in Basel)
Client:	Canton Basel-Stadt, Department of civil services and environment,
	Planning department, Münsterplatz 11, 4001 Basel
Dates:	project planning and construction 1989–2003

KLINIKUM 1, CANTONAL HOSPITAL RENOVATION

Spitalstrasse 21, 4056 Basel | Tram 11, Bus 34 36 38: Kantonsspital

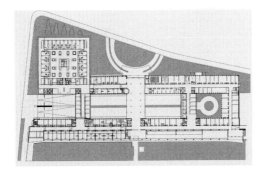

Ground-floor plan with new annex by Gmür/Vacchini (top left)

Basel's university hospital was fully renovated over the course of fourteen years. Silvia Gmür and Livio Vacchini were the signatory architects of a consortium of architects. Hermann Baur, the architect of the original building, completed in 1945, placed particular emphasis on the human scale. Respecting this philosophy, the architects have nevertheless thoroughly modernized the building. The massive complex is 180 metres long, with two wings (three storeys and nine storeys high). Thanks to sliding fire doors, the unbroken interior lines of the building can be fully experienced. Beauty in form and material was paramount in all the upgrades (sanitary and electrical installations, signage, transportation, furnishings). The architects added the new women's clinic (project 11) to the west wing.

Entrance atrium

The nine-storey main building

Architect:	Gmür / Vacchini, Pflüggässlein 3, 4001 Basel
Client:	Kantonsspital Basel, Hebelstr. 32, 4031 Basel
	Canton Basel-Stadt, Department of civil services and environment,
	Planning department, Münsterplatz 11, 4001 Basel
Dates:	project planning 1994–1999, construction 2000–2003

WOMEN'S CLINIC WITH OPERATING THEATRES

Spitalstrasse 21, 4031 Basel | Tram 11, Bus 30 33: Frauenspital | Bus 36 38: Kantonsspital

Waiting area in the corridor next to facade

Although Gmür/Vacchini added the new Women's Clinic of the university to the structure designed by Hermann Baur (project 10), the cube with the simple glass facade has the presence of a detached building. The architects attached a square with a side length of 40 metres and three storeys to the west wing of the historic ensemble, organizing the comprehensive spatial programme around two courtyards and restoring the ideal, rectangular geometry of the ensemble on the Schanzenstrasse elevation. The facade, composed of filigree concrete rods and floor-high glass panels, transforms the interior spaces (in combination with the light falling into the building from the courtyards) into patient- and staff-friendly environments. The furnishings, prototypes designed by the architects, the high-quality exposed concrete and a colour palette ranging from lime-green to yellow and blue (especially in the flooring) correspond to the high requirements for hygiene, and also reflect a design approach that is a harmonious blend of skilful execution and aesthetic-psychological perception.

Elevation seen from the intersection of Schanzenstrasse/Spitalstrasse

Ground plan with courtyards

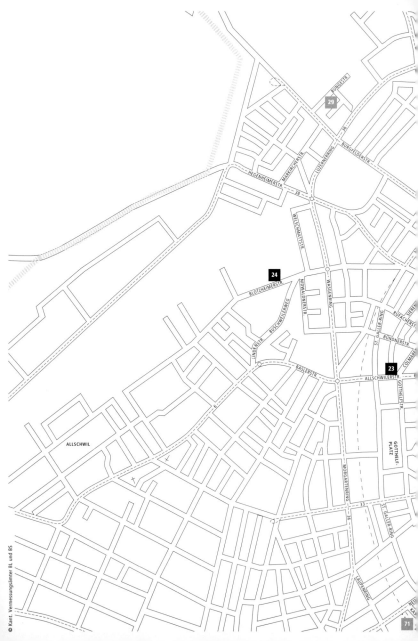

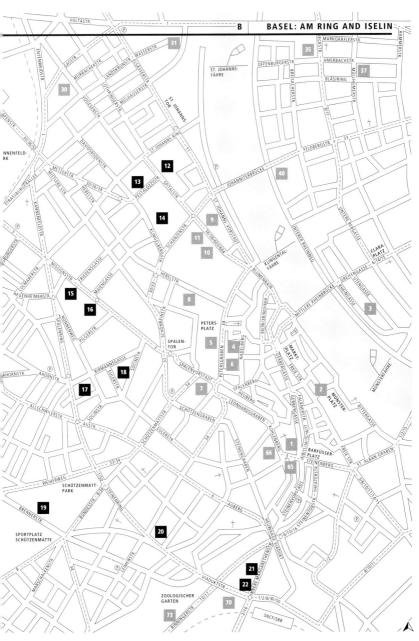

Architect:	Diener & Diener, Henric Petri-Strasse 22, 4010 Basel
Client:	Canton Basel-Stadt, Department of civil services and environment,
	Planning department, Münsterplatz 11, 4001 Basel
Dates:	construction 1992–1996

VOGESEN SCHOOL

St. Johanns-Ring 17/Spitalstrasse, 4056 Basel | Tram 11: St. Johanns-Tor |
Bus 30 33 36 38 603 604: Frauenspital

Standard floor plan, second to fourth floor

The first phase of the Vogesen School construction by Diener & Diener was completed in 1994, the second phase in 1996. Increased student enrolment and school reforms led to higher standards for the school facilities in Basel from the 1980s onwards. In 1994, Diener & Diener's project was the first new school building to be constructed in the city in twenty years. The elegant four-storey tiered-concrete building accommodates a total of forty classrooms, a gym, and extensive ancillary facilities. The entranceway, as well as the entire access area, are finished in Onsernone granite from the Ticino Mountains. The facade is composed of green-tinted poured concrete slabs. The classrooms, with windows reaching almost from floor to ceiling, have an inviting atmosphere.

East-west section

Facade on courtyard side

Classroom on second floor

Architect:	Fierz & Baader, Basel
	Since 1995 Fierz Architekten, Leimenstrasse 76, 4051 Basel
	and Stefan Baader, Güterstrasse 144, 4002 Basel
Client:	Canton Basel-Stadt, Department of civil services and environment,
	Planning department, Münsterplatz 11, 4001 Basel
Dates:	competition 1989, construction 1993–1996

INSTITUTE OF ANATOMY, UNIVERSITY OF BASEL

Pestalozzistrasse 20, 4056 Basel | Bus 30 33 36 38 603 604: Frauenspital | Tram 11: St. Johanns-Tor

The dissection hall

Section of lecture and dissection hall (left), of Anatomical Museum (centre), and facade of historic building (right).

The asymmetric cube of the lecture and dissection hall

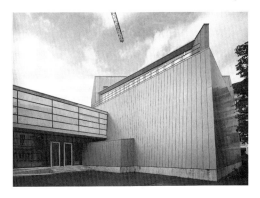

The Institute of Anatomy at the University of Basel has been extensively transformed, renovated, and enlarged by a new addition. Architects Peter Fierz and Stefan Baader placed an asymmetric cube next to the Art Nouveau building from 1921, lowered the new lecture hall (and the dissection facility above it) into the ground, and created new rooms for the Anatomical Museum. The former lecture hall was converted into a library and a photo studio. Exposed concrete, granite, and oak and beech parquet flooring demonstrate the high quality of the materials used in the construction. To create a column-free open space for the new lecture hall, the architects laid a massive brace across the cube, whose square plan was modified into a diamond shape. This project is a prime example of successful dialogue between the old and the new.

Architect:	Andrea Roost, Steinerstrasse 36, 3006 Bern
	Associates Andreas Kaufmann and Heiri Tannenberger
Client:	Canton Basel-Stadt, Department of civil services and environment,
	Planning department, Münsterplatz 11, 4001 Basel
Dates:	graduate study commission 1987/1988, construction 1996–2000

BIO-PHARMAZENTRUM OF THE UNIVERSITY

Klingelbergstrasse 50–70, 4056 Basel | Bus 30 36 38: Metzerstrasse | Bus 33: Frauenspital

Ground floor

The facade of the new Pharmazentrum on Klingelbergstrasse is covered in a square grid of exposed concrete rods. This ideal geometry and the nine-storey height have redefined the streetscape: the structure is a self-assured focal point for all neighbouring buildings. The labyrinthine entrance hall, reaching from the ground floor to the third floor, is the core element of the building. The foyer is executed in expertly handled exposed concrete and finished in granite. With columns, stairs, galleries, and landings, the design has resulted in a space that opens up sightlines in all directions and from all perspectives, reminiscent of Piranesi's fantastical etchings.

Facade on Klingelbergstrasse

Three-storey-high entrance atrium

Architect:	Fierz & Baader, Basel
	Since 1995 Fierz Architekten, Leimenstrasse 76, 4051 Basel
	and Stefan Baader, Güterstrasse 144, 4002 Basel
Client:	Youth Care Association, Missionsstrasse 47, 4055 Basel
Dates:	project planning and construction, 1992–1993

TRAINING WORKSHOP

Missionsstrasse 47, 4055 Basel | Tram 3: Pilgerstrasse | Tram 1: Hegenheimerstrasse

West facade

Fierz & Baader placed a long, slender cube into a courtyard behind a building on Missionsstrasse. The plain louvred facade across two floors clearly signals the use of the three-storey building as a training workshop for apprentices in carpentry. The design is in the tradition of the modular pattern used for industrial architecture. The bare fabric is divided by generous ribbons of windows. At the northern end, the uppermost row of windows and the vertical stairwell combine to create a fully glazed corner, which frames and structures the facade. The free-standing breadth of the building to the south features a narrow vertical window slit across the full height of the building. The windows in the concrete wall follow the additive principles of a Donald Judd sculpture.

BASEL: AM RING AND ISELIN

Stairwell with glass skin

Ground floor

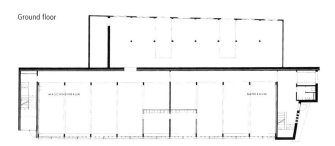

Architect:	Urs Gramelsbacher, Steinengraben 36, 4051 Basel
Client:	Protestant Baptist Congregation, Missionsstrasse 37, 4055 Basel
Dates:	construction 1993–1995

RESIDENTIAL BUILDING WITH MEETING HALL

Missionsstrasse 37, 4055 Basel | Tram 3: Pilgerstrasse | Tram 1: Hegenheimerstrasse

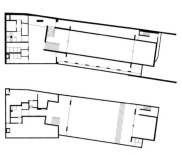

Floor plan of meeting hall (below) and mezzanine

Facade on Missionsstrasse

For the Baptist congregation in Basel, Urs Gramelsbacher designed a residential building with a meeting hall. On the narrow and angled lot, the low-lying volume of the hall abuts the four-storey residential unit. The floor plans are based on a 6 metre × 6 metre grid that creates harmonious proportions in the rooms and on the facade. The prayer hall lies on the same level as an underground car park would and is structured like a basilica. Light falls into the space through a skylight and a light well, which is positioned much like an apse. The hall – designed for a capacity of 200 people – has an understated and serene atmosphere. There are no overt sacred symbols, merely an abstract cross composed of four window squares at the far end.

Entrance area of residential building

Architect:	Atelier Gemeinschaft (Michael Alder, Hanspeter Müller, Roland Naegelin),
	St. Johanns-Vorstadt 3, 4056 Basel
Client:	Basel Association for the Mentally Handicapped, Mostackerstrasse 14, 4051 Basel
Dates:	project planning 1995/1996, construction 1997

HOME FOR THE MENTALLY HANDICAPPED

Birmannsgasse 37, 4055 Basel | Tram 1: Birmannsgasse | Tram 3, Bus 33: Spalentor

Ground floor

Facade on Birmannsgasse

On Birmannsgasse the architects' cooperative designed a building for the Association for the Mentally Handicapped. This five-storey building is a bright, friendly, and attractive structure, unusual for an institutional building. The materials are especially beautiful: the facades are characterized by finely formed exposed concrete and large glazed surfaces framed in oak. The communal and dining areas on the raised ground floor have light-coloured French limestone floors. The window sills and counters in both kitchens are made of sanded and polished granite. The furnishings, designed by the architects in collaboration with two specialty design shops, are equally elegant. The panoramic view from the fifth-floor patio is a visual treat.

Facade overlooking garden

Architect:	Esther Brogli & Daniel Müller, Burgweg 16, 4058 Basel
	Associates Rosmarie Schwarz and Adrian Weber
Client:	Gesellschaft für das Gute und Gemeinnützige (GGG), Basel;
	Willi+Carola Zollikofer Foundation, Basel
Dates:	competition 1987/1988, construction 1988–1991

LINDENHOF NURSING HOME

Socinstrasse 30/Eulerstrasse, 4051 Basel | Tram 3, Bus 30 33: Spalentor | Tram 1 6, Bus 50: Brausebad

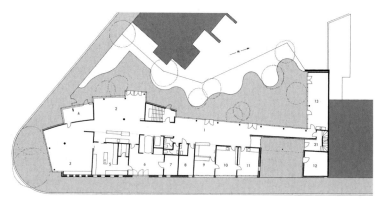

Ground floor

On the periphery of the downtown core, architects Esther Brogli and Daniel Müller built a home for twenty-seven seniors. The linear structure, with rhythmically arranged windows, follows the contour of the street on one side of the acute-angled lot composed of trapezoids and triangles. On the courtyard side, balconies, ribbons of windows on the ground floor, and the moderate height – a mere three storeys – emphasize the human scale of this architecture, as does Samuel Eigenheer's landscape design. The former Lindenhof Nursing Home, which used to occupy this site, was nondescript and went largely unnoticed. The new building has retained the name but is far more expressive, introducing an urban accent to this residential neighbourhood.

BASEL: AM RING AND ISELIN

Facade on Euler- and Socinstrasse

Architect:	Barcelo Baumann Architekten, Hegenheimerstrasse 98, 4055 Basel
Client:	Canton Basel-Stadt, Department of civil services and environment,
	Planning department, Münsterplatz 11, 4001 Basel
	Verein offener Pavillon Schützenmattpark, Schützenmattpark 1, 4051 Basel
Dates:	competition 2000, project planning and construction 2002–2003

PAVILION IN SCHÜTZENMATTPARK

Schützenmattpark 1, 4054 Basel | Tram 1, Bus 33 34: Schützenhaus | Tram 8: Bundesplatz

East elevation

The Schützenmattpark, created in 1898/99, contained a music pavilion which was destroyed by vandalism. The architects Barcelo Baumann won the competition for a successor building. The result is a multi-functional building with a café restaurant, facilities for activities and events organized by local associations, a site for concerts and cultural events, and a new focal point in the park. The solid larch structure clad in spruce siding is composed of four spatial corner elements covered by a single roof. Large glass doors open the interior onto the park in the summer months and emphasise the central location of the building, newly set up in the middle of the park triangle. From a distance (seen from the north) the pavilion has the appearance of a ship that seems to float on the green of the lawn.

Facade overlooking the square

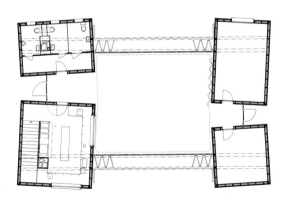

Ground plan

Architect:	Alioth Langlotz Stalder Buol, Klingental 15, 4058 Basel
	with Diener & Diener, Henric Petri-Strasse 22, 4010 Basel
Client:	Holbeinhof Foundation, Leimenstrasse 67, 4051 Basel
Dates:	construction 2000–2002

"HOLBEINHOF" SENIORS RESIDENCE AND NURSING HOME

Leimenstrasse 67, 4051 Basel | Tram 6, Bus 33 34: Schützenmattstrasse | Tram 8: Zoo Bachletten

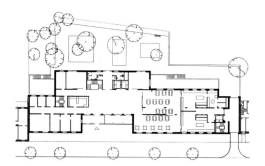

Ground floor

When the Leimenstrasse was constructed around 1870, it was designed as a suburban boulevard with rows of two- and three-storey homes. With its five storeys, the Holbeinhof seniors residence and nursing home, planned and constructed by the architects Alioth Langlotz Stalder Buol in collaboration with Diener & Diener, is a symbol of the urbanization of the now inner-city location. The home for 111 seniors is a Jewish-Christian pilot project that is unique in Switzerland. The ground floor contains the reception area, living-, dining- and other communal spaces, with the openness and generosity of an intimate hotel setting. The clever layout of the building form creates a piazza in the exterior space and provides the interior with a varied and interesting floor plan. Twelve planted squares in front of the facade bearing the names of the months in Yiddish and German declare the interfaith philosophy of the project.

Facade on Leimenstrasse

Stairwell with skylight

Architect:	Wilfrid and Katharina Steib, Unterer Rheinweg 56, 4057 Basel
Client:	Canton Basel-Stadt, Department of civil services and environment,
	Planning department, Münsterplatz 11, 4001 Basel
Dates:	construction 1991–1995

PUBLIC PROSECUTOR'S OFFICE AND MUNICIPAL JAIL

Binningerstrasse 21/Innere Margarethenstrasse 18, 4054 Basel | Tram 1 2 8 16: Markthalle | Tram 6 10 16 17: Heuwaage

Corridor between public prosecutor's office (right) and municipal jail (left)

Ground floor

Facade on Binningerstrasse

The new building for the public prosecutor's office and the municipal jail stands on a challenging site: between the streets that surround the property, the terrain drops by as much as the equivalence of three storeys. The shape of the lot is composed of two rectangles, one trapezoid, and several triangles. On this property the architects erected a building with a total of 26 000 square metres in floor space. The structure is divided into two sections, which correspond to its separate functions as prosecutor's office and jail. The former is housed in the section at the bottom of the property, while the jail section is integrated into the hillside. An elegant, convex curved facade of more than 100 metres in length is one of the outstanding architectural features of this building.

Architect:	Richard Meier & Partners, 475 Tenth Avenue, New York, NY 10018
	Project management Bernhard Karpf
Client:	Credit Suisse, Zurich
Dates:	project planning 1990–1993, construction 1995–1998

EUREGIO OFFICE BUILDING

Viaduktstrasse 40–44, 4051 Basel | Tram 1 2 8 16: Markthalle | Tram 6 10 16 17: Heuwaage

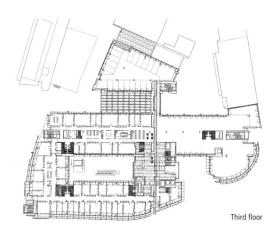

Third floor

Richard Meier's first building in Switzerland is clad in white aluminium sheeting. The eleven-storey structure (five storeys on the south-facing Viaduktstrasse and eleven on the west-facing Binningerstrasse) has a total floor space of over 35 000 square metres. The white of the walls and the grey of the granite floor combine to create a professional and harmonious atmosphere in the office spaces. The location of the building is noteworthy. Diagonally across from Meier's new building lies a residential development from 1915 in traditional "fin de siècle" style. On the valley side, the new building is neighbour to a structure from 1934 in the International Style, while the UBS training and conference centre (project 70) across the street exemplifies the new simplicity in contemporary architecture.

Facade on Viaduktstrasse

Conference area on third floor

Architect:	Herzog & de Meuron, Rheinschanze 6, 4056 Basel
	Project management Annette Gigon
Client:	Horat Generalunternehmung AG, Schützenmattstrasse 39a, 4051 Basel
Dates:	competition 1985, construction 1987–1988

RESIDENTIAL AND OFFICE BUILDING

Allschwilerstrasse 90 / Sierenzerstrasse / Colmarerstrasse, 4055 Basel | Tram 6: Allschwilerplatz | Bus 36: Morgartenring

Second to fifth floor

The first large building designed by Herzog & de Meuron to be built in Basel is located on Allschwilerstrasse. The rectangular lot is slightly curved along its length. The main facade follows this curve, as does the facade that overlooks the courtyard. Access balconies lead to eight 3.5-room and twelve 4.5-room apartments on all five upper floors. The ground floor features generous windows and is predominantly reserved for retail use. The pretinted concrete slabs of the facade point to a characteristic element in later projects by this creative architectural team: the sculptural external skin.

BASEL: AM RING AND ISELIN

Facade on Allschwiler- and Colmarerstrasse

Access balconies on courtyard facade

Architect:	Peter Zinkernagel, Bartenheimerstrasse 17, 4055 Basel
Client:	Canton Basel-Stadt, Department of civil services and environment,
	Planning department, Münsterplatz 11, 4001 Basel
Dates:	project planning 1993, construction 1994–1995

WASGENRING SCHOOLHOUSE EXPANSION

Blotzheimerstrasse 82, 4055 Basel | Bus 36: Buschweilerweg | Bus 38: Thomaskirche | Tram 6: Lindenplatz

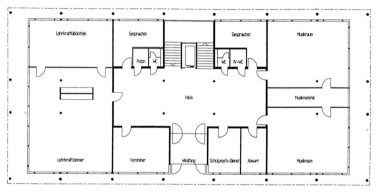

Ground floor

The large school complex on Wasgenring dates from 1951. It was recently expanded with a new addition designed by Peter Zinkernagel. Bruno and Fritz Haller's original concept for the multi-stream elementary school was an ensemble of free-standing pavilions, which were completed in two building phases: 1951–1955 and 1958–1962. Zinkernagel chose to pick up on the established pattern by placing a slender slab along the north-south axis. He successfully combines New Building aesthetics with contemporary building technology and a 1990s philosophy of education by means of large glass surfaces, simple floor plans, and a green-tinted glazed facade between the ribbons of windows. The artist Renate Buser was commissioned to etch the glazing on the east side.

B | BASEL: AM RING AND ISELIN

The new school building (left) with
its predecessors from 1962

Site plan

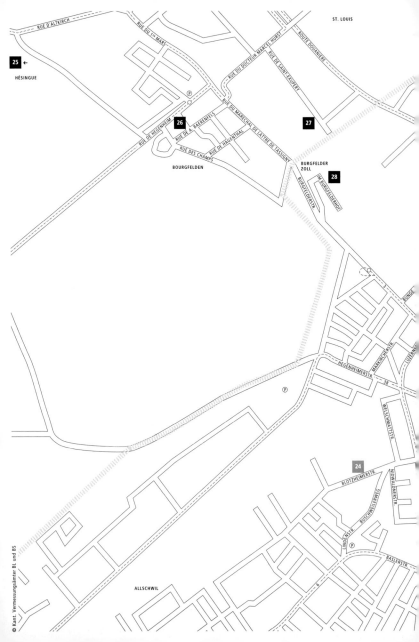

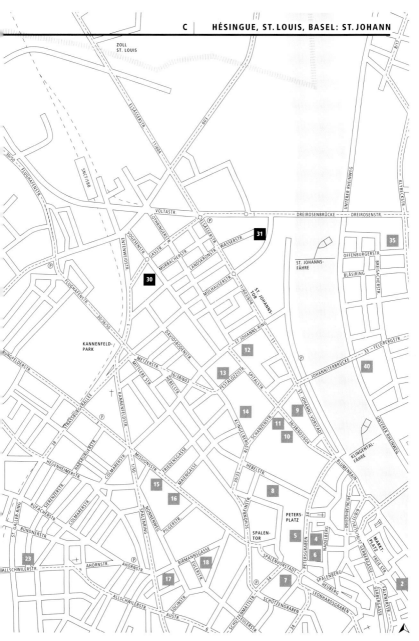

Architect:	Berrel Architekten, Missionsstrasse 35a, 4055 Basel
	Associate Martin Stettler
Clients:	R. and H. Berrel-Argast, Hésingue
Dates:	construction 1996–1997

SINGLE-FAMILY HOUSE

42, rue de Saint-Louis, F-68220 Hésingue | Bus 601: Hésingue Centre |
(Tram 3: Burgfelden Grenze and a 30min. walk)

Ground floor

The single-family house designed by Berrel Architekten in Hésingue owes its spatial organization to the unusual conditions of the site. In order to stay within the prescribed building height, the two-storey structure was lowered into the ground, with access provided from sunken courtyards. Single-storey cubes were added on the east and west sides of the main structure, which is oriented north-south. These wings are accessible at ground level from the outside and via small stairs on the inside. This resulted in a cross-shaped ground plan. The open space on the ground floor is made even more visually inviting by floor-to-ceiling windows on all sides and sliding glass doors. Every angle offers exhilarating views into the large garden.

Main facade overlooking the garden

Central staircase

Architect:	Daniel Stefani & Bernard Wendling, 4a, rue de Huningue, F-68300 St. Louis
Client:	Municipality of St. Louis, City Hall, F-68300 St. Louis
Dates:	construction 1992–1993

KINDERGARTEN AND CLUB HOUSE

rue Anne de Gohr/rue de A. Baerenfels, F-68300 St. Louis | Bus 601 602: Bourgfelden Centre | Tram 3: Burgfelden Grenze | Bus 30 50: Friedrich Miescher-Strasse

The gym bathed in light

The kindergarten against the backdrop of 1960s housing blocks

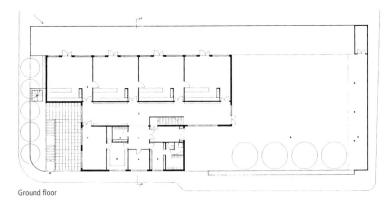

Ground floor

Daniel Stefani & Bernard Wendling built a kindergarten in Burgfelden, a central neighbourhood in St. Louis dominated by large housing blocks from the 1960s and a busy traffic artery. A roofed arbor, with slate slabs mounted to the inside, protects against noise and emissions. It also serves as a drawing surface for the children. In the large gym, the architects arranged the windows in a zigzag pattern. This results in optimal natural light and creates an invigorating, even euphoric, feeling in the interior space. The basement level contains meeting rooms for local clubs and associations. This kindergarten building is topped by a roof terrace.

Architect:	Herzog & de Meuron, Rheinschanze 6, 4056 Basel
	Project management Eric Diserens
Client:	Bürgerspital Basel, Leimenstrasse 62, 4051 Basel
Dates:	project planning 1989/1990, construction 1992–1993

PFAFFENHOLZ SPORTS COMPLEX

5, rue de St. Exupéry, F-68300 St. Louis | Tram 3: Burgfelden Grenze |
Bus 30 50: Friedrich Miescher-Strasse

Site plan: the Swiss border is to the right

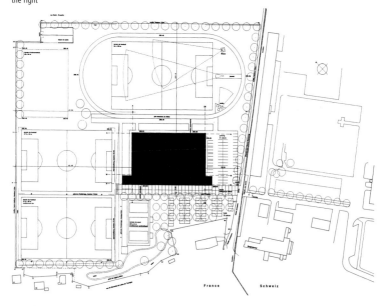

C | HÉSINGUE, ST. LOUIS, BASEL: ST. JOHANN

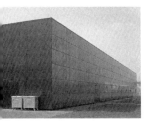

The sculptural glass skin

Exposed concrete surfaces define the interior

Herzog & de Meuron's sports complex, featuring a large indoor gym and an open-air oval track, is located at the border between Switzerland and France. Since the service ducts are hidden behind the glass facade, the interior is exposed concrete. The entrance area is dominated by a clear-span roof that runs the full length of the building and is its most monumental feature. The interior and exterior are linked by light: daylight creates bright channels throughout and vistas that stretch up to 70 metres. The gym floor was sunk into the ground, allowing for an external shape that is almost flat. The facade glazing, tinted dark with screen prints, gives the building an almost sacred air.

Architect:	Planning: Herzog & de Meuron, Rheinschanze 6, 4056 Basel
	Construction planning: Proplaning AG, Burgfelderstrasse 211, 4025 Basel
Client:	REHAB Basel AG, Im Burgfelderhof 40, 4055 Basel
Dates:	competition 1998, project planning 1998–1999, construction 1999–2002

REHAB – SWISS CENTRE FOR PARAPLEGICS, BASEL

Im Burgfelderhof 40, 4025 Basel | Tram 3: Burgfelden Grenze | Bus 30 50: Friedrich Miescher-Strasse

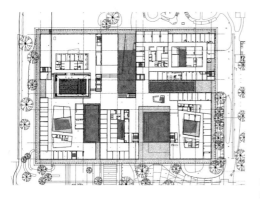

Floor plan of 2nd storey with main entrance (top centre)

On the border between Switzerland and France, the new Swiss Centre for Paraplegics (REHAB) has been realized on a lot of 144 by 86 metres. In this building created for the rehabilitation of paraplegics and brain-injured, Herzog & de Meuron emphasise the horizontal. The structure comes alive through the use of concrete, timber and glass, making it very bright in the interior and giving it a very light appearance on the exterior. The architects have structured the facade as well as the network of paths connecting the 9500 m² floor area in the building with four large and four small courtyards. As a result there is an abundance of light channels and numerous rooms with aquatic plants (designed by landscape architect August Künzel). In this western city, the new building appears like the pavilion of an East-Asian temple or palace ensemble. The Pfaffenholz sports complex (project 27) is located on the other side of the border fence.

South-west elevation

View from the foyer on the upper storey into two courtyards

Architect:	Michael Alder, St. Alban-Vorstadt 24, 4052 Basel
	Associate Hanspeter Müller; now Atelier Gemeinschaft,
	St. Johanns-Vorstadt 3, 4056 Basel
Client:	Basel civil servants pension fund, Clarastrasse 13, 4051 Basel
	Neue Wohnbaugenossenschaft, Basel
Dates:	competition 1989, construction 1991–1993

LUZERNERRING HOUSING DEVELOPMENT

Bungestrasse 10–28, 4055 Basel | Tram 3, Bus 36: Luzernerring

Verandahs and balconies
on Bungestrasse

Standard floor plan, second to fifth floor

Michael Alder created a "residential street" between Luzernerring and Bungestrasse with six units and ninety-eight apartments. The spacious apartments are intended predominantly for large families. Nearly every room opens onto outside spaces such as balconies or enclosed porches, which are generously proportioned for a social housing project at 20 square metres. The ground-floor units have small gardens. Each of the six buildings includes a common room complete with kitchen on the ground floor, a covered bicycle stand in the courtyard, a sandbox, and a fruit tree. Residents also enjoy access to the 200-metre-long rooftop covered in gravel, yet another outdoor space.

Architect:	Erny, Gramelsbacher, Schneider
	Since 1993 Erny & Schneider, St. Alban-Vorstadt 68a, 4052 Basel
	and Urs Gramelsbacher, Steinengraben 36, 4051 Basel
Client:	Christoph Merian Foundation, Basel; Helvetia Patria Insurance Group, Basel
Dates:	competition 1987, construction 1989–1991

IM DAVIDSBODEN HOUSING DEVELOPMENT

Gasstrasse/Vogesenstrasse, 4056 Basel | Tram 1: Gasstrasse/Bahnhof St. Johann |
Tram 11, Bus 603 604: Voltaplatz

Site plan

With 155 apartments, three kindergartens, clinics, studios, workshops, a library, and an auditorium, the Davidsboden development has changed the face of St. Johann, a neighbourhood characterized by a blend of residential and industrial use. Close to the French border, it creates an urban marker as Diener & Diener's Hammer 1 development (project 38) did ten years earlier. The four- to six-storey structure meets the requirements of social life in an urban setting by providing wintergardens and creating a child-friendly environment. Glazed projections create rhythmical divisions in the large volume. Fairface brickwork and linear forms emphasize friendliness and serenity. The covered walkways fulfil two roles: circulation paths within the development and outdoor meeting places.

Facade on Gasstrasse

View into a courtyard

Architect:	Quintus Miller & Paola Maranta, Schützenmattstrasse 31, 4051 Basel
Client:	Canton Basel-Stadt, Department of civil services and environment,
	Planning department, Münsterplatz 11, 4001 Basel
Dates:	competition 1996, construction 1999–2000

VOLTA SCHOOL

Wasserstrasse 40/Mülhauserstrasse, 4056 Basel | Tram 1: Novartis Campus | Tram 11: Mülhauserstrasse | Bus 603 604: Voltaplatz

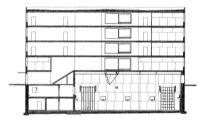

East-west section

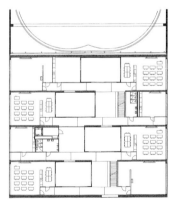

Third to fifth floor

Facade on Wasserstrasse

When a fuel depot located on busy Mülhauserstrasse was demolished, space became available for a new building for the Volta School. Architects Quintus Miller and Paola Maranta moved the entrance to Wasserstrasse, an adjoining dead-end street, to make it safer for children. Four open light wells are central features of the structure. They are distributed across four of the five storeys in a zigzag formation. Large glazed surfaces open up views into all the interiors, the rooms that are not located along the outside of the building are thus provided with sufficient daylight. An atrium for school recess is located just inside the main entrance. All common rooms are located above the two-storey gym.

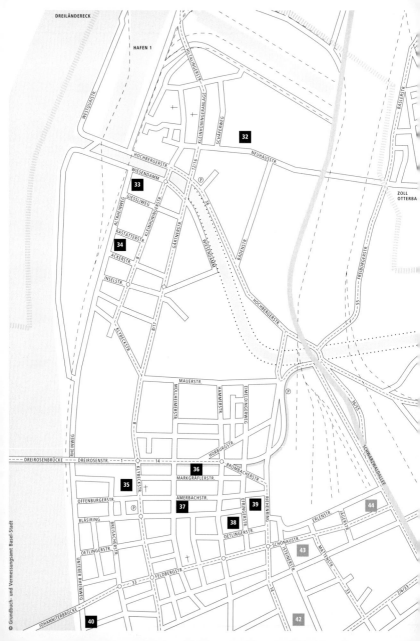

D | BASEL: KLEINHÜNINGEN, KLYBECK, MATTHÄUS

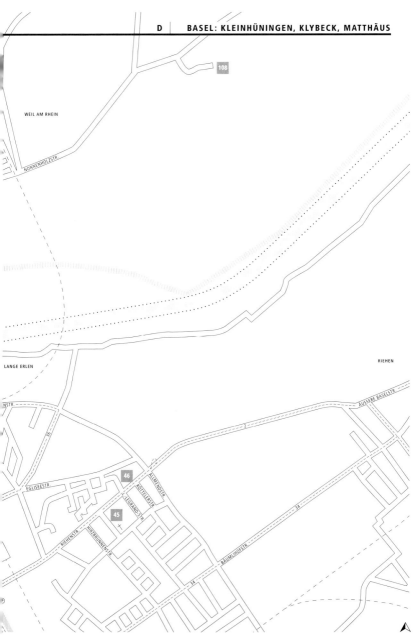

Architect:	Stefan Baader, Güterstrasse 144, 4002 Basel
Client:	Industrial Works Basel (IWB), Margarethenstrasse 40, 4053 Basel
Dates:	construction 1998–1999

IWB CENTRAL STORAGE

Neuhausstrasse 31, 4057 Basel | Tram 8, Bus 36: Kleinhüningen | Bus 12 16: Weilerweg

The passage for cable drums

The new IWB central storage depot is located near the Rhine harbour. The complex lies directly on Südquaistrasse and in close proximity to a wet dock. Architect Stefan Baader designed the required space by building three separate volumes. The four-storey main structure rises from an impressive ground plan (18 m × 80 m). With its large concrete surfaces and narrow ribbons of windows, it is a monolithic presence on the site. Parallel to it lies the second structure, an open warehouse notable for its airy shed-roof construction. Finally, there is a 100-metre passage for cable drums whose square section has the visual impact of an alpine cavern.

East elevation

North-south section

Architect:	Wilfrid und Katharina Steib, Unterer Rheinweg 56, 4057 Basel
	in collaboration with Bruno Buser & Jakob Zaeslin, Basel
Client:	Basel civil servants pension fund, Clarastrasse 13, 4051 Basel
Dates:	competition 1980, construction 1983–1986

WIESENGARTEN HOUSING DEVELOPMENT

Wiesendamm / Altrheinweg / Giessliweg, 4057 Basel | Tram 8, Bus 12 16 36: Kleinhüningen

Third to sixth floor

With 168 apartments ranging in size from 1.5 to 5.5 rooms, the Wiesengarten development was the most important project of its kind in the 1980s in the northern section of Basel. Studio and commercial spaces were included, stipulating mixed use from the very beginning. The complex consists of seventeen buildings situated on a tributary of the Rhine (the Wiese), with Kleinhüningen harbour nearby and a short bicycle ride away from a large nature and recreation area (Lange Erlen). The architects varied the building heights and set architectural circle segments against the facade, giving the large volume a pleasing rhythm and structure. The interiors are finished to very high standards.

The housing development seen from the north with the facade overlooking the Wiese River

A residential street on the courtyard side

Architect:	Ackermann & Friedli, Schützenmattstrasse 43, 4051 Basel
	Since 1999 Ackermann Architekt
Client:	Canton Basel-Stadt, Department of civil services and environment,
	Planning department, Münsterplatz 11, 4001 Basel
Dates:	project development and planning 1994, construction 1995–1996

ACKERMÄTTELI SCHOOL

Rastatterstrasse 32, 4057 Basel | Tram 8: Wiesenplatz, Inselstrasse | Bus 36: Kleinhüningen

Access at ground-floor level

The neighbourhoods in the north and north-west of Basel are residential and industrial districts. Architects Ackermann & Friedli erected a new school in this sector of the city, in the Klybeck neighbourhood. It is situated in a grassy area bordered by trees and separated from the Rhine by a train track and docks. The new Ackermätteli School provides not only a valuable new educational facility for the district, it also improves the urban layout of the area: the L-shaped building frames the heterogeneous residential buildings to the east, creating a cohesive block. The rows of windows in the four-storey building produce a tranquil geometry and transform the grassy area into a small park. The architecture is an important urban marker at this location.

Third and fourth floors

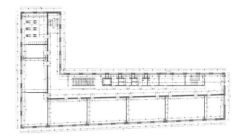

Facade on Altrheinweg

Architect:	Morger & Degelo, Spitalstrasse 8, 4056 Basel
	Associates Marianne Kempf and Lukas Egli
Client:	Canton Basel-Stadt, Department of civil services and environment,
	Planning department, Münsterplatz 11, 4001 Basel
Dates:	construction 1990–1996

DREIROSEN SCHOOL EXPANSION

Breisacherstrasse 134 / Klybeckstrasse 111–115, 4057 Basel | Tram 1 8 14: Dreirosenbrücke

Facade overlooking Dreirosen Park

On Klybeckstrasse, next to the small park at the Dreirosenbrücke, Morger & Degelo have expanded an existing school and erected a new residential building. On the street side, the residential building relates to the five-storey structure of a Neo-Baroque church by August Hardegger (1902). The architects retained the vertical volume of the original school building designed by K. Leisinger (1906), but have gained an additional floor by decreasing the floor height at each level. A large underground gym beneath the schoolyard as well as workshop spaces and studios for art courses are linked to the original structure by a 90-metre-long enclosed colonnade, which also shields the school from the noisy street. There are many large bands of windows. The residential building consists of twenty-nine units ranging from two to four rooms in size.

Courtyard with lit squares from the underground gym

Site plan: the new buildings are to top left

Architect:	Wilfrid and Katharina Steib, Unterer Rheinweg 56, 4057 Basel
Client:	Ecumenical Foundation Horburg-Marienhaus, Basel
Dates:	competition 1992, construction 1993–1996

MARIENHAUS NURSING HOME

Horburgstrasse 54/Markgräflerstrasse 47/49, 4057 Basel | Tram 1 8: Dreirosenbrücke | Tram 14: Brombacherstrasse

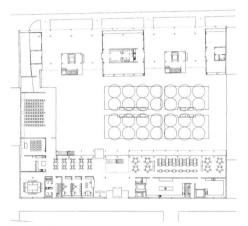

Ground-floor plan

Architects Wilfrid and Katharina Steib have designed a nursing home and adjacent housing, a pilot project in Swiss geriatrics. The clients are the two main Christian churches. Twenty units are apartments for families who will work in the nursing home; twenty more are assigned to seniors and/or people with varying degrees of disability. The architects have distributed the extensive room requirements across two building units (linked by a connecting wing) and arranged these sections around an inner courtyard. All open-air areas of the housing complex (balconies, patios, covered walkways) face the courtyard. The seniors' residence has a bright reception area reminiscent of a hotel lobby. Abundant use of wood and glass has created a building where old and young can experiment with new forms of living together.

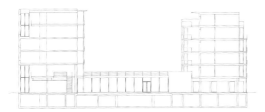

East-west section

Courtyard facade of nursing home

Architect:	Morger & Degelo, Spitalstrasse 8, 4056 Basel
	Associate Lukas Egli
Client:	Canton Basel-Stadt, Department of civil services and environment
	Planning department, Münsterplatz 11, 4001 Basel
Dates:	competition 1989, project planning and construction 1990–1993

HOUSING CO-OP

Müllheimerstrasse 138/140, 4057 Basel | Tram 8: Bläsiring | Bus 33: Hammerstrasse

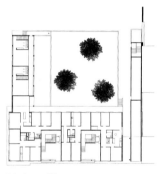

Raised ground floor

The housing co-op on Müllheimerstrasse had a similar impact in north-west Basel as did the nearby Hammer 1 housing development (project 38). The twenty-six four- to five-room apartments are distributed across one raised ground floor and five upper floors. The kindergarten is located on the "base" floor, just below the raised ground floor. Reddish brown panels of cement-bound wood lend a sculptural tone to the structure and enter into a dialogue with the brickwork of the neighbouring buildings, which date back to the late nineteenth century. At the same time, the wraparound balconies and patios on the upper floors established a new typology for residential buildings in the city. Since the "windows" onto these balconies or patios are in fact floor-to-ceiling French doors, the interior of the building is suffused with light.

Elevator shaft and stairwell

Architect:	Diener & Diener, Henric Petri-Strasse 22, 4010 Basel
Client:	Baselland civic servants pension fund, Arisdörferstrasse 2, 4410 Liestal
Dates:	construction 1978–1981

HAMMER 1 HOUSING DEVELOPMENT

Hammerstrasse / Bläsiring / Efringerstrasse, 4057 Basel | Tram 14: Musical-Theater |
Bus 33: Hammerstrasse

Site plan with new building
(left) and the historic buildings on
Oetlingerstrasse (right)

The apartments, studios, and retail shops created by Diener & Diener in the late 1970s in a small housing development catapulted Basel's contemporary architecture to an international level. The five-storey structure, bordered on three sides by different streets – thereby nearly defining a city block – was designed with six-storey-high projections at two intersections. Square wood-framed windows create tranquil geometrical facades. Most of the apartments have wintergardens on the courtyard side, supported by a bold metal construction. The studio buildings in the courtyard are accessible via covered walkways. The architects treated the facade in an unusually poetic manner by using painted bricks.

Facade and wintergardens on courtyard side

Architect:	Diener & Diener, Henric Petri-Strasse 22, 4010 Basel
Client:	Baselland civic servants pension fund, Arisdörferstrasse 2, 4410 Liestal
Dates:	planning and construction 1980–1985

HAMMER 2 HOUSING DEVELOPMENT

Efringerstrasse / Amerbachstrasse / Riehenring, 4057/58 Basel | Tram 14, Bus 33: Riehenring

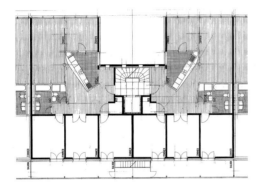

Third to fifth floor on Riehenring

The Matthäus neighbourhood, developed in the last quarter of the nineteenth century as a residential, commercial, and industrial district, shifted decisively towards modernity with the construction of Diener & Diener's Hammer 1 and Hammer 2 housing developments. Another high-impact residential structure was created to the north (project 44), and the new Fair Hall (project 42) is located on the same street (Riehenring). Only a few city blocks separate Hammer 2 from a new residential building (project 37). Diener & Diener divided the facade of the large building into squares. The linear floor plans are generous in size and the building also features large patios and roof gardens. Retail stores and a supermarket help to give the development the feeling of a neighbourhood.

The projection at the corner of
Amerbachstrasse and Riehenring

Architect:	Wilfrid and Katharina Steib, Unterer Rheinweg 56, 4057 Basel
Client:	Community of heirs Unterer Rheinweg, Basel
Dates:	competition 1993, construction 1994–1996

RESIDENTIAL BUILDING ON THE WATER'S EDGE

Unterer Rheinweg 48–52, 4057 Basel | Bus 33: Erasmusplatz | Tram 8: Feldbergstrasse

Facade on the Rhine

Wilfrid and Katharina Steib have erected a six-storey building with forty-eight units (3- to 5.5-room apartments and three penthouse units) on grounds formerly occupied by an 1878 villa. In 1910, a large residential building in the Art Nouveau style was erected on the lot adjoining the villa grounds. At the time, the construction considerably increased the density of this central location. The facade of the new building is completely glazed on the sides that overlook the Rhine and the park. All units extend across the full depth of the building (15 m, or 17 m including the projecting balconies) and are extremely bright. The windows, framed in Oregon pine, overlook the Rhine in what is an optimal southern exposure and provide near-perfect noise protection.

Living areas overlooking the river

North-south section

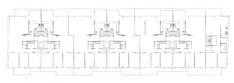

Second to sixth floor

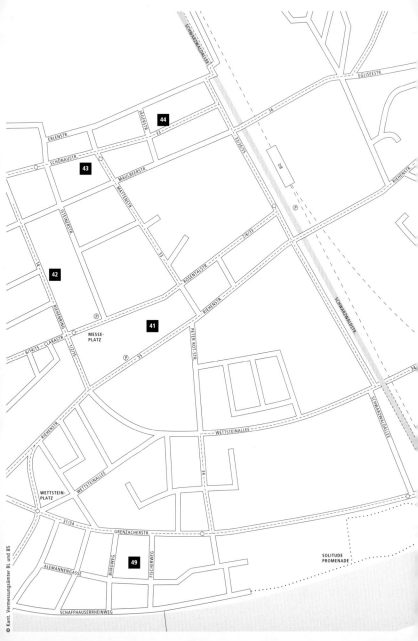

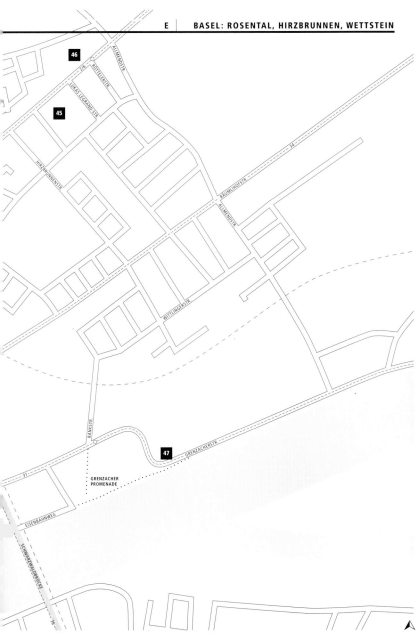

E | BASEL: ROSENTAL, HIRZBRUNNEN, WETTSTEIN

Architect:	Cooperation Morger & Degelo AG, Spitalstrasse 8, 4056 Basel
	with Marques AG, Rankhofstr. 3, 6006 Lucerne
	Project management: Erich Offermann
	Execution: Manfred Kunz
Client:	Swiss Prime Site AG, represented by Credit Suisse Asset Management
Dates:	competition 1998, project planning 1999–2000, construction: 2000–2003

HIGH-RISE FOR BASEL FAIR

Messeplatz, 4021 Basel | Tram 1 2 6 14 15: Messeplatz | Bus 34: Claraplatz

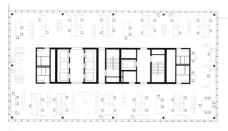

Floor plan

With the completion of the 105-metre-tall high-rise in 2003, Basel has become home to the tallest building in Switzerland (previously the tallest building was the Sulzer high-rise in Winterthur, erected in 1967). The architects Morger, Degelo and Marques have housed the thirty-one upper storeys in an unembellished steel-and-glass cube, projecting the third and fourth floors elegantly into the street space to the east. The new tower is connected to Hans Hofmann's cylindrical courtyard building (1953/54) by a 60-metre-long reflecting pool. The wooded Rosental area to the east and the rigorously designed town square of the fair grounds to the south are improved by the glass tower, transformed into a green and urbane site. The high-rise continues the tradition of modern towers, begun by Ludwig Mies van der Rohe (860 Lake Shore Drive Apartments in Chicago, 1948–51/ Seagram Building in New York, together with Philip Johnson, 1954–58). The new fair hall (project 42) is close by.

BASEL: ROSENTAL, HIRZBRUNNEN, WETTSTEIN

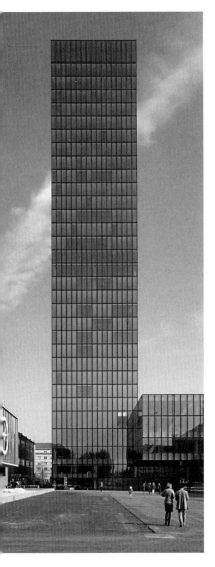

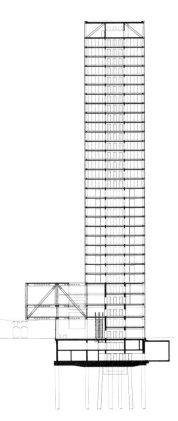

East-west section

Elevation as seen from the Messeplatz

Architect:	Theo Hotz, Münchhaldenstrasse 21, 8034 Zürich
Client:	Basel Fair, Messeplatz 1–3, 4058 Basel
Dates:	competition 1996, construction 1998–1999

NEW FAIR HALL

Messeplatz 1 / Riehenring / Isteinerstrasse, 4058 Basel | Tram 2 6 14 15: Messeplatz |
Bus 33: Gewerbeschule

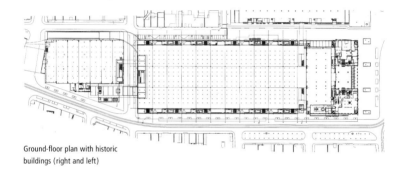

Ground-floor plan with historic
buildings (right and left)

Facade on Riehenring

Ground floor of the large hall

Theo Hotz's new Fair Hall is proof that industrial architecture on a large scale (90 m wide, 210 m long, and some 20 m high) can indeed be elegant. The structure may be described as two halls, one on top of the other, creating grand room heights (10 m and 8 m, respectively) and monumental interiors. The architect added a glass and steel structure to the original building (1923–1927). The new design has been as much a surprise to the exhibitors as it has to the fair visitors. The original building had a closed facade of dark clinker bricks. With its fully glazed end walls, the new building resembles a giant shop window. Since Basel's fairground is located in a residential and commercial district, this architecture – clearly visionary both from a technical and an aesthetic perspective – sets new standards for all future construction in the district. The new fair tower (project 41) ist the most recent addition.

Architect:	Diener & Diener, Henric Petri-Strasse 22, 4010 Basel
	Landscape design: August Künzel
Client:	Baukonsortium Stücki, Henric Petri-Strasse 22, 4010 Basel
Dates:	construction 2000–2002

STUDIO HOMES, APARTMENT BUILDING AND HOTEL

Atelierhäuser Isteinerstrasse 90-96, Dorinth Hotel Schönaustrasse 10 and 31–35 |
Tram 1: Riehenring | Bus 33: Mattenstrasse

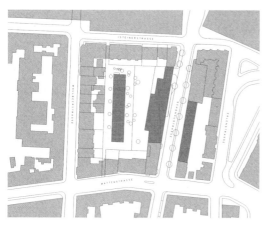

Site plan with the Isteinerstrasse (top) and the Mattenstrasse (bottom)

For the 11 studio homes on the Isteinerstrasse, Diener & Diener employed the motif of the monumental staircase (here across two storeys) in housing construction (see projects 2, 86). In proximity to the fair, the single-family homes, a five-storey apartment building and a hotel represent new developments arranged with great precision on lots that were formerly dedicated to industrial uses. Linear access and plans, large to oversized fenestration and spatial arrangements set an urban milestone at this location. Together with the two large housing structures to the south (projects 38, 39), the architects have defined the culture of building in this district for twenty-five years.

The studio homes seen from the east

The continuous staircase in the studio homes

Architect:	Proplaning, Burgfelderstrasse 211, 4025 Basel
Client:	Basel civic servants pension fund, Clarastrasse 13, 4051 Basel
Dates:	planning and construction 1997–1999

HOUSING DEVELOPMENT

Schönaustrasse/Erlenstrasse, 4058 Basel | Bus 33: Mattenstrasse | Tram 2 6, Bus 36 55: Badischer Bahnhof

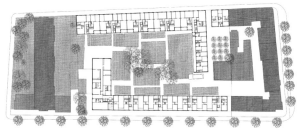

Ground floor

The two L-shaped buildings arranged by Proplaning to frame a 3000-square-metre courtyard have a total facade of 500 metres. The imposing volume is pushed by the two projections into an adjoining courtyard, which is surrounded by late-nineteenth-century buildings. The six-storey blocks contain 163 apartments ranging from 2.5 to 4.5 rooms in size, three workshops, a kindergarten, and a café/restaurant, thereby creating a neighbourhood within the neighbourhood. Fifty percent of the apartments have loggias. The floors are finished in oak or cast stone, and there is the added luxury of floor heating in these units.

E | BASEL: ROSENTAL, HIRZBRUNNEN, WETTSTEIN

Facade overlooking courtyard

Architect:	Christian Dill, Pfluggässlein 3, 4001 Basel
	Associates A. Dalla Favera and R. Brunner
Client:	Canton Basel-Stadt, Department of civil services and environment,
	Planning department, Münsterplatz 11, 4001 Basel
Dates:	competition 1991/1992, planning and construction 1992–1997

HOUSING AND THERAPY FACILITY

Riehenstrasse 300, 4058 Basel | Tram 2 6: Eglisee

The pavilion-style residential building

For a pilot project at the university's department of psychology, Christian Dill has designed a housing and therapy facility for mentally and physically handicapped adults. The complex consists of a two-storey residential building and a three-storey building for therapy and meetings. The buildings are almost completely faced in Douglas fir. The residential building follows the slight angle of the northern boundary on the park-like property. This elongated building is arranged around two courtyards, allowing for maximum light from all sides. The therapy and meeting building is located next to the high traffic road, and serves to shield the complex against noise and exhaust fumes. On this facade, the most public side of the complex, the architect arranged all the windows according to internal light requirements. The abstract character of the facade reminds one of a score for solo instrument.

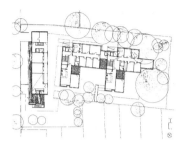
Second floor

Main building on Riehenstrasse

Architect:	Diener & Diener, Henric Petri-Strasse 22, 4010 Basel
Client:	Migros-Genossenschaft Basel, Thiersteinerallee 71/73, 4053 Basel
Dates:	construction 1996–1997

EGLISEE SUPERMARKET

Riehenstrasse 315, 4058 Basel | Tram 2 6, Bus 39: Eglisee

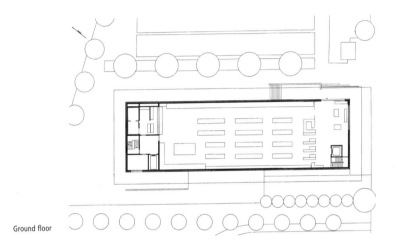

Ground floor

Diener & Diener built a supermarket on Riehenstrasse that breaks the mould in terms of typological design. The clean geometry of the rectangular shell is repeated in the interior, where the rhythm is echoed in the arrangement of shelves and aisles, introducing calm into a world overloaded with consumer goods. The large horizontal windows, reaching from the top of the shelves to just below the ceiling, are also part of this precise arrangement. With their material harmony, the poured concrete slabs of the facade create a new focal point in the heterogeneous architectural environment. Because of its use, the building signals openness and an urban character.

Entrance area on Riehenstrasse

Architect:	Michael Alder, St. Alban-Vorstadt 24, 4052 Basel
	Associate Roland Naegelin; now Atelier Gemeinschaft,
	St. Johanns-Vorstadt 3, 4056 Basel
Client:	Canton Basel-Stadt, Department of civil services and environment,
	Planning department, Münsterplatz 11, 4001 Basel
Dates:	project planning 1991/1992, construction 1993–1995

RANKHOF STADIUM

Grenzacherstrasse 351, 4058 Basel | Bus 31: Sportzentrum Rankhof

The column-free circulation area

The new Rankhof Stadium was created as part of the overall refurbishment of Basel's largest sports complex on the right bank of the Rhine. It is a functional building with a capacity of 15 000; the elegant grandstand has a total of 900 covered seats. In addition, the stadium houses twenty-four changing-rooms, club rooms, and a restaurant. Beneath the tiered grandstand is a column-free circulation area approximately 100 metres in length. On the other sides of the field, the seating is constructed of stacked 18-tonne prefabricated components, with seven steps between each landing. Concrete is the predominant material in the sports complex. The galvanized metal railings match the range of greys in the plastic-coated seats of the grandstand. The rear wall consists of a glass skin with black metal frames.

The grandstand

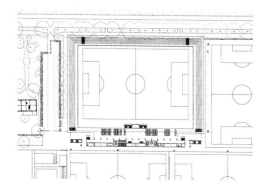

Plan

Architect:	Mario Botta, Via Ciani 16, 6904 Lugano
	Project management and site supervision Georg Steiner
	in collaboration with Baucontrol AG, Basel
Client:	F. Hoffmann-La Roche AG, Grenzacherstrasse 124, 4058 Basel
Dates:	project planning 1993, construction 1994–1996

JEAN TINGUELY MUSEUM

Grenzacherstrasse 210, 4058 Basel | Bus 31 36: Tinguely Museum

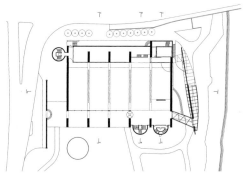

Ground floor

A small park called Solitude and Mario Botta's museum dedicated to the artist Jean Tinguely are located between a highway and office buildings designed for Hoffmann-La Roche. The architect used a windowless rear wall to shield the museum against noise and the park against exhaust fumes. The museum overlooks the Rhine on the south side and the park on the west side. Botta is an architect who loves the grand gesture: here, he has created a generously proportioned building around an 1800-square-metre central hall. All the circulation routes and visual axes are linear. An adjoining older building houses the museum's administration. The architect placed an enclosed footbridge along the Rhine in front of the museum, laying the river at the visitor's feet.

E | BASEL: ROSENTAL, HIRZBRUNNEN, WETTSTEIN

Footbridge and Rhine facade

Architect:	Diener & Diener, Henric Petri-Strasse 22, 4010 Basel
Client:	Warteck Invest AG, Grenzacherstrasse 79, 4058 Basel
Dates:	construction 1994–1996

WARTECKHOF DEVELOPMENT

Grenzacherstrasse 62/64/Fischerweg 6–10/Alemannengasse 33–37, 4058 Basel
Bus 31 34: Rosengartenweg | Tram 2 15: Wettsteinplatz

Floor plans of the two historic buildings (left) and the new buildings (right)

Two historic buildings were preserved on the property of the former Warteck Brewery. Diener & Diener added a residential building (eighty-one units of up to five rooms per unit and live-in studios) and an office and retail block. For the housing block and its brickwork facade the architects entered into a dialogue with the original industrial building; the other new building is located on a traffic artery through the eastern part of the city and takes a definite contemporary stance with a facade composed of green concrete slabs. The historic buildings were complemented with new buildings in such a manner as to create a shifting landscape of open spaces, passages, and sightlines – thus achieving correspondences and rhythm. The redeveloped area comes across as more compact and thus, by definition, more urban.

View from fifth floor to the west

The former mashhouse (right) with
new buildings

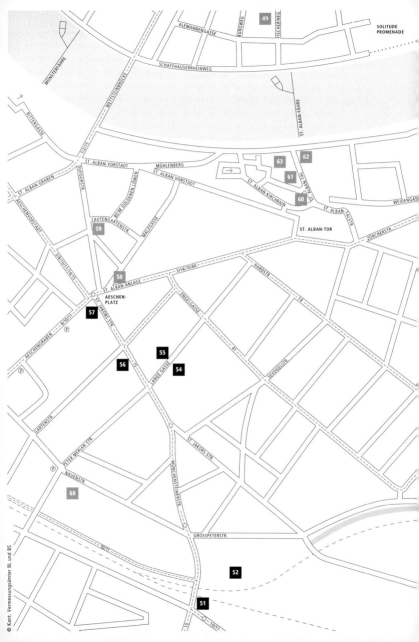

Architect:	Scheiwiller & Oppliger, Basel
	Since 1999 Dolenc Scheiwiller Architekten, St. Jakobs-Strasse 54, 4052 Basel
Client:	Christoph Merian Foundation, St. Alban-Vorstadt 5, 4051 Basel
Dates:	original bathhouse 1898, expansion 1929, competition 1988,
	renovation and reconstruction 1990 and 1993–1994

BREITE BATHING STATION ON THE RHINE

St. Alban-Rheinweg 195, 4052 Basel | Tram 3, Bus 36 70 80: Breite

Steel structure from the
nineteenth century

F | BASEL: BREITE AND ST. ALBAN

The Rhine bathing station with a view upriver

Section

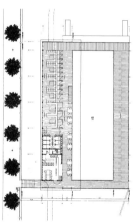

Floor plan of entrance storey

A public bathhouse "in" the Rhine was renovated and reconstructed by architects Scheiwiller & Oppliger. Eighty percent of the original steel construction from 1898 was built above water. While a 1929 addition was largely demolished, any other components that were still useful were salvaged, while adding everything that is required to satisfy modern demands. The most notable changes are a small restaurant, toilet facilities, updated wiring, and oak flooring. The structure features a louvred facade and is once again a pavilion above water. Even in its new "reincarnation," the defining element of the building is the nineteenth-century engineered metal construction.

Architect:	Herzog & de Meuron, Rheinschanze 6, 4056 Basel
	Project management Philippe Fürstenberger
Client:	Federal Swiss Railroad, Luzerne
Dates:	project planning 1995/1996, construction 1998–1999

CENTRAL SWITCH-YARD

Münchensteinerstrasse 115, 4052 Basel | Tram 10 11: Münchensteinerstrasse | Tram 15: Grosspeterstrasse

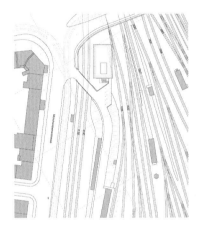

Site plan

In 1994 architects Herzog & de Meuron built a switch-yard for the Federal Swiss Railroad with a copper ribbon facade. It lies hidden to the east of the city. In 1999, another switch-yard was created for the same client on the edge of the city's downtown in a very exposed location. It features the same facade and, at 26 metres, rises to a height of approximately ten storeys. Set on the tracks, the ground plan is an uneven trapeze that mutates into a rectangle by the time it reaches the roof contour. These geometric forms merge rhythmically into one another across the full height of the building and the structure twists elegantly upward in a slightly convex movement. The architecture is both expressive and minimalist. Moreover, it has the presence of an outdoor sculpture.

F | BASEL: BREITE AND ST. ALBAN

Building as seen from the tracks (top) and from Münchensteiner bridge

Architect:	Bürgin & Nissen in association with Zwimpfer Partner
	Since 2001 Nissen & Wentzlaff Architekten, St. Alban-Vorstadt 80, 4052 Basel
	Zwimpfer Partner, St. Alban-Anlage 66, 4052 Basel
Client:	PTT General Management, Bern
Dates:	project planning and construction 1984–1989

SWISSCOM

Grosspeterstrasse 18, 4052 Basel | Tram 15: Grosspeterstrasse

Facade on Grosspeterstrasse

F | BASEL: BREITE AND ST. ALBAN

Swisscom (foreground) with high-rises in the background

The telecommunications centre on Grosspeterstrasse is surrounded by a constant flow of automobile and rail traffic. The calm volumes of this building, in some sections with elegant ribbons of windows, reflect the subtlety and care with which Bürgin & Nissen (chief architects) and Zwimpfer Partner approached the planning for this project. The architects divided the spatial requirements into two separate volumes which follow the slope in two steps to the large railway-yard of the train station. Upon completion, the new building and the Lonza high-rise (1960–1962) were the only structures to occupy this site on the edge of the city. Since then, other important architectural markers have been added, especially the new switch-yard on the other side of the tracks (project 51) and the Peter Merian House on the same thoroughfare (project 68).

Architect:	Herzog & de Meuron, Rheinschanze 6, 4056 Basel
Client:	Miteigentümergesellschaft (MEG) Basel, Winterthur Life Insurance Group,
	Swiss Accident Insurance (SUVA) Lucerne, Basel civil servants pension fund
Dates:	project planning 1996, 1998, construction 1998–2002

ST. JAKOB PARK (soccer stadium, shopping centre, retirement home)

St. Jakobs-Strasse 395, 4052 Basel | Tram 14, Bus 36: St. Jakob

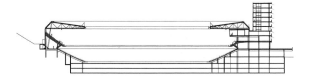

North-south section

Taking the train from the SBB station in the east/south-east direction is to follow a Herzog & de Meuron route: in short succession, you will travel past the central switch-yard (project 51), its slightly older predecessor (also clad in copper), a locomotive depot and, after the St. Jakob Park stop, the stadium of the same name. At roughly 200 metres, the longitudinal stands of the new sports arena are almost as long as the station platform. The roof above the stands, which is parallel to the St. Jakobs-Strasse, is connected to a retirement home and the comprehensive spatial programme for the infrastructure required for sports and other events in a tall slim building. The basement and ground floor accommodate a shopping centre. The soccer stadium is designed in the British style without an oval for track and field. The 32 000 seats are compactly distributed across four sections: the playing field is within close reach from all sides. The retirement home is clad in concrete panels; the stadium in domed synthetic components, which resemble a quilted jacket. In contrast to 1954, when a stadium for the soccer World Cup in Switzerland was built in the same location, the density of the street space has been increased and given a more urban appearance.

F | BASEL: BREITE AND ST. ALBAN

Facade on the St. Jakobs-Strasse

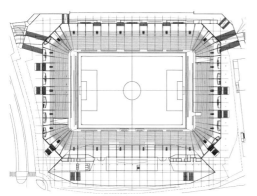

Ground plan

Architect:	Proplaning, Burgfelderstrasse 211, 4025 Basel
Client:	Sport-Toto-Group, Lange Gasse 20, 4052 Basel
Dates:	construction 1997

SPORT-TOTO CONVERSION

Lange Gasse 20, 4052 Basel | Tram 3 8 10 11 14, Bus 41 70 80: Aeschenplatz | Tram 15: Denkmal

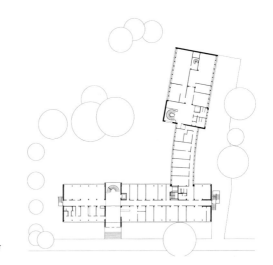

Ground floor

The administration building of the Sport-Toto-Group remained at its original site. But the architects from Proplaning stripped the F. Rickenbacher building (1957) down to its shell, making access wings more spacious. State-of-the-art technology has resulted in a far more transparent facade, which was simply suspended in front of the concrete grid construction. This has enlarged all of the office spaces to some degree. Electrical and building services are integrated into the ceilings, slightly lowering the ceiling height. The beauty of the original materials and the elegance of the 1950s architecture are still reflected in the central winding staircase, which has been preserved in its original state. The conversion has simply improved and optimized a historic situation.

Facade on Lange Gasse

Architect:	Burckhardt+Partner AG, Dornacherstrasse 210, 4002 Basel
Client:	Winterthur Life Insurance Group, Winterthur
Dates:	project planning 1997, construction 1998–2000

OFFICE BUILDING

Lange Gasse 15, 4052 Basel | Tram 3 8 10 11 14, Bus 41 70 80 : Aeschenplatz | Tram 15: Denkmal

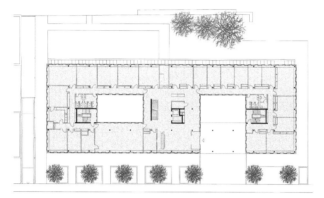

Ground floor

Architects Burckhardt Partner designed an office building for Gellert, a residential neighbourhood. At 22 by 65 metres and four storeys, the fabric encloses a massive volume that is nevertheless cleverly integrated into its environment by being slightly set back from the frontage line and by the ground floor sunken. A supporting framework of 5.4 by 5.4 metres is the central structural element that allows for great flexibility of use and also gives the entire shape an air of tranquillity and clarity. The interior is characterized by two open light wells. The interior courtyard to the north leads to a generous entrance and lobby area; together, the courtyards provide natural light for almost all utility areas, while the offices, situated exclusively along the peripheral facade, benefit from optimal daylight through the abundant glazing. The facade is composed of wood and aluminium elements that break the surface into smaller units, creating a rhythm like a musical score.

View into one of the light wells

Elevation on Lange Gasse

Architect:	Herzog & de Meuron, Rheinschanze 6, 4056 Basel
	Project management Kurt Lazzarini
Client:	Swiss Accident Insurance (SUVA), Luzerne
Dates:	project planning 1988, construction 1991–1993

SUVA HOUSE

St. Jakobs-Strasse 24/Gartenstrasse 53/55, 4052 Basel | Tram 3 8 10 11 14 15, Bus 41 70 80 : Aeschenplatz

Facade on St. Jakobs-Strasse

On the edge of downtown, Herzog & de Meuron have converted and enlarged an office building in Basel and added a residential section: the SUVA House has become one of Basel's most elegant and striking architectural features. To integrate the original 1950 building with the new addition, both structures were encased in a glass skin on the street facades. The opening of the office windows is now computer-regulated. On the courtyard side, the stone facade of the old building meets the wood facade of the new addition. A new café has been named after the Icarus bas-relief above the original 1950 main entrance. To generate a photographic wallpaper, the architects used an archival Icarus image from the sixteenth century (by Pieter Brueghel the Elder).

Glass skin for historic building (left) and adjoining new residential building

Architect:	Mario Botta, Via Ciani 16, 6904 Lugano
	Project management and building supervision
	in partnership with Burckhardt Partner, Dornacherstrasse 210, 4053 Basel
Client:	Swiss Bank Association, Basel
Dates:	1986, construction 1990–1995

BIS ADMINISTRATION BUILDING

Aeschenplatz 1, 4052 Basel | Tram 3 8 10 11 14 15, Bus 41 70 80: Aeschenplatz

Facade on Aeschenplatz

On Aeschenplatz, Mario Botta created a bank building whose 28-metre height and imposing volume surpass his cathedral in Paris Evry. The rotunda building is the architect's largest building north of the Alps. Among the many international architects who have designed buildings in Basel during the last decade, Botta has been the most controversial. And yet the powerful half-circle design is an architectural archetype common to the Mediterranean landscape. At the edge of the city's downtown, the building sets a strong urban accent and the boulevard, inspired in part by Botta's structure, has already expanded in the direction of the train station. The most characteristic element of the building is an enclosed light well that rises from the ground floor to the roof. Into this open space artist Felice Varini's suspended circles are extremely precise and equally sensuous.

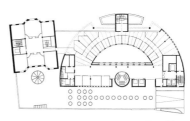

Ground floor

Enclosed atrium

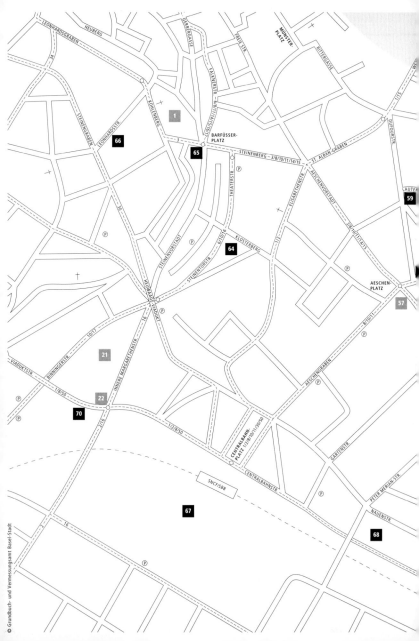

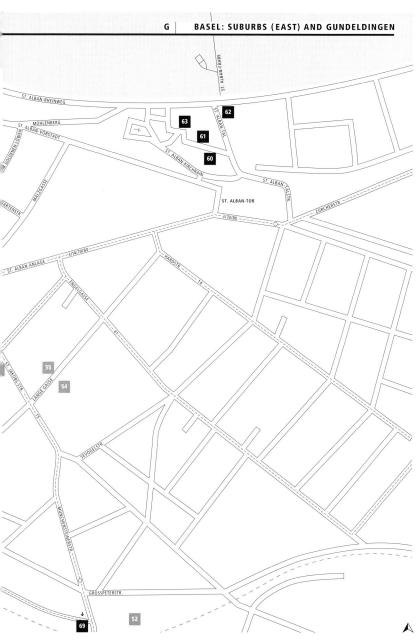

Architect:	Bürgin Nissen Wentzlaff, St. Alban-Vorstadt 80, 4052 Basel
	Since 2001 Nissen & Wentzlaff Architekten
Client:	Pax Life Insurance Group, Basel
Dates:	competition 1988/1989, construction 1992–1994 and 1995–1997

PAX INSURANCE ADMINISTRATION BUILDING

Aeschenplatz 13, 4052 Basel | Tram 3 8 10 11 14 15, Bus 41 70 80: Aeschenplatz

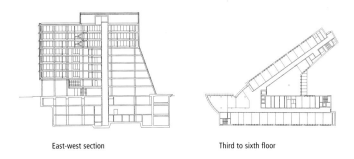

East-west section   Third to sixth floor

A new administration building for the Pax Insurance Group has been erected on Aeschenplatz. The building by Bürgin Nissen Wentzlaff includes a striking glass tower that is a complementary counterpoint to Mario Botta's rotunda building in the same square (project 57). Glass, steel, and the brickwork in the facade are the dominant materials. The tiered facade of the V-shaped design responds to the historic neighbourhood. On the boulevard side, nine storeys rise in an austere form. On the north-west side, where a neighbourhood of small lots leads to the historic downtown, the height has been reduced to three storeys in harmonious correspondence to the surroundings. The predominant materials are stone and wood, that is, granite and beech. Lamps and handrails are prototypes designed by the architects.

Entrance hall

Facade on Aeschenplatz

Architect:	Diener & Diener, Henric Petri-Strasse 22, 4010 Basel
Client:	Life Insurance Group of Basel, Aeschengraben 21, 4051 Basel
Dates:	competition 1987, construction 1990–1994

PICASSOPLATZ BUSINESSCENTER

Lautengartenstrasse 6/Dufourstrasse, 4052 Basel | Tram 3 8 10 11 14 15, Bus 41 70 80: Aeschenplatz | Tram 2 15: Kunstmuseum

Second to fifth floor

On the far side of Picassoplatz, Diener & Diener erected an administration building for the Life Insurance Group of Basel. The complex in three sections (five, six, and eight storeys) occupies a trapezoidal lot. The building creates a new urban anchor for this prominent central location. One of the three sections is almost a perfect cube: an ideal geometry. The facade is polished green granite. Granite – albeit, in white and black – is also the material used in Luciano Fabro's large sculpture installation which surrounds the entire complex. The new building stands in a neighbourhood with an important architectural history, including Otto Rudolf Salvisberg's First Church of Christ, Scientist (1935/1936) and the art museum designed by Rudolf Christ, Paul Büchi, and Paul Bonatz (1929–1936).

South section through connecting wing

Facade on Dufourstrasse

Architect:	Michael Alder, St. Alban-Vorstadt 42, 4052 Basel
	Partner Roland Naegelin; now Atelier Gemeinschaft,
	St. Johanns-Vorstadt 3, 4056 Basel
Client:	Residents' Cooperative St. Alban-Tal, Basel
Dates:	project planning 1984/1985, construction 1986

CONVERSION OF INDUSTRIAL ARCHITECTURE

St. Alban-Tal 42, 4052 Basel | Tram 3: St. Alban-Tor | Tram 2 15: Kunstmuseum

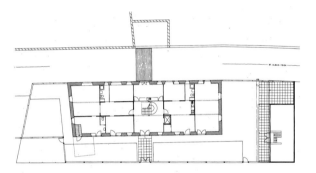

Ground-floor plan

Michael Alder has fully renovated and converted a nineteenth-century building whose historic use was to provide living quarters for paper mill workers, as well as drying rooms for the mill. In place of the original support structure of vertical elements along the central longitudinal axis, a new circulation zone has been inserted through the centre of the building. This creates the structural conditions required for the building's new and exclusively residential use while preserving the original girder structure. Externally, the conversion has also maintained a visual link to the original architecture through rows of equidistant window axes and a wooden envelope of Douglas fir facade strips. This building is a prime example of a trend that was unthinkable only a few years ago: the will to invest such care into existing buildings that are in poor repair.

G | BASEL: SUBURBS (EAST) AND GUNDELDINGEN

The building after being stripped to the shell (top)

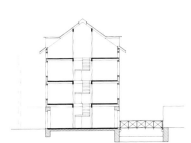

Plan after refurbishment (left) and new facade

Architect:	Urs Gramelsbacher, Steinengraben 36, 4051 Basel
Client:	National Insurance Group, Steinengraben 41, 4051 Basel
Dates:	construction 1997–1999

RESIDENTIAL BUILDING

St. Alban-Tal 38a, 4052 Basel | Tram 3: St. Alban-Tor | Tram 2 15: Kunstmuseum

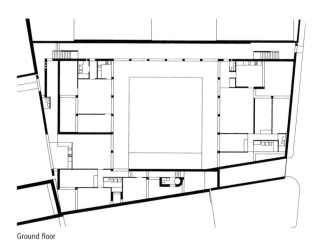

Ground floor

On the last free parcel of land remaining in the St. Alban valley-neighbourhood on the Rhine between Romanesque monastery architecture and the late medieval city wall, Urs Gramelsbacher constructed a new residential building with three- and five-room apartments. The two-storey-high structure is oriented towards a central courtyard (17×17 m). Exposed concrete is the dominant material. The courtyard fountain creates a veil of water flowing through a slit (10 m ×4 cm) in the concrete. The water collects in a glass-bottomed basin, which is in fact the ceiling of an underground car park designed to provide parking for all neighbouring houses. Wall openings integrate the new building with its environment.

Street facade

Courtyard

Architect:	Diener & Diener, Henric Petri-Strasse 22, 4010 Basel
Client:	Christoph Merian Foundation, St. Alban-Vorstadt 5, 4052 Basel
Dates:	competition 1982, construction 1984–1986

RESIDENTIAL BUILDING WITH CRAFT STUDIOS

St. Alban-Rheinweg 94/96, 4052 Basel | Tram 3: St. Alban-Tor | Tram 2 15: Kunstmuseum

Facade overlooking the Rhine with
medieval city wall (left)

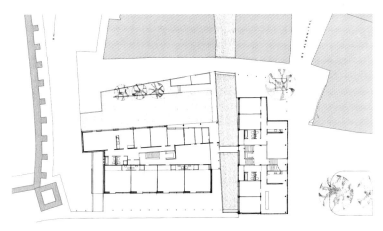

Ground floor

In the historic St. Alban valley (see project 63) Diener & Diener have built an exposed building on an undeveloped stretch along the Rhine. With its clean design, serial window arrangement, and the sculptural effect of the facade, the building is deliberately contemporary in tone. It is especially remarkable from the perspective of urban planning as the architecture interacts so harmoniously with its historic surroundings. The adjoining city wall along the riverbank dates from the late Middle Ages. And the buildings – used as paper mills from 1453 and 1478 onwards – bear witness to the city's early industrial development. The historic dialogue, present in several areas of the city, is at its best in this location (see projects 60 and 61).

Architect:	Wilfrid and Katharina Steib, Unterer Rheinweg 56, 4057 Basel
Client:	Museum of Contemporary Art, the Emanuel Hoffmann Foundation, Basel, and the Public Art Collection in St. Alban-Tal, Basel
Dates:	construction 1977–1980

MUSEUM OF CONTEMPORARY ART

St. Alban-Rheinweg 60, 4052 Basel | Tram 3: St. Alban-Tor | Tram 2 15: Kunstmuseum

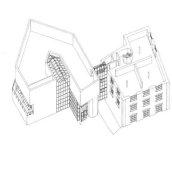

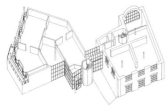

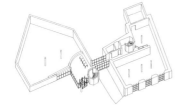

Axonometric of museum (top),
of second floor (middle),
and of ground floor

G | BASEL: SUBURBS (EAST) AND GUNDELDINGEN

Facade with main entrance

In 1980 Basel became home to a new Museum of Contemporary Art with an exhibition space of 2 800 square metres. In the same year, twenty-seven museums were under construction or projected for construction in Germany. The theatrical impulse of many of these architects is barely felt in Basel. For this museum, a former paper mill was partially demolished and the remaining volume nearly doubled through the addition of a new building. The architects designed the connecting structure and the entrance area in steel and glass – in keeping with the factory windows, which were preserved. The ground floor of the new building is partially below ground, such that the building heights vary only slightly. The large windows provide excellent light conditions, and the top floor of the new building is conceived as an open space with a full-ceiling skylight.

Architect:	Schwarz-Gutmann-Pfister, Elisabethenstrasse 28, 4010 Basel
	Projektleitung: Stephan Nyffeler
Client:	Canton Basel-Stadt, Department of civil services and environment,
	Planning department, Münsterplatz 11, 4001 Basel
Dates:	project planning: 1996–1999, construction 1999–2002

NEW SCHAUSPIELHAUS

Steinentorstrasse 7, 4051 Basel | Tram 6 10 16 17: Heuwaage | Tram 2: Kirschgarten

East-west section

In the facade of the new Schauspielhaus (theatre), the inner city has gained a display window of some 300 square metres. The architects erected the building on a trapezoidal lot between the Klosterberg and the Steinentorstrasse, and arranged the stage-/backstage as well as the audience areas along the street sides. Glass, exposed concrete and timber are the dominant materials visible to the visitors. With 500 seats, which can change position to accommodate six different stage variations ranging from "viewing box" to "arena," the theatre is an ideal complement to the city's principal theatre (two stages with seating for 1200 and 330, respectively). The architects have deftly accommodated the opulent spatial programme comprising dressing rooms, make-up rooms, props, sound, lighting, workshops, shop and building services, in the two side wings and in the basement.

G | BASEL: SUBURBS (EAST) AND GUNDELDINGEN

Facade on the Klosterberg side

Facade with main entrance on Steinentorstrasse

Architect:	Diener & Diener, Henric Petri-Strasse 22, 4010 Basel
Client:	M. Diener, Basel
Dates:	construction 1994–1995

RESIDENTIAL BUILDING WITH OFFICE AND RETAIL SPACE

Steinenvorstadt 2/Kohlenberg 1, 4051 Basel | Tram 3 6 8 11 14 15 16: Barfüsserplatz | Tram 10: Theater

The corner building on Barfüsserplatz

Ground-floor plan (top), standard floor plan, fourth to sixth floor

Section from Kohlenberg perspective

On Barfüsserplatz, Diener & Diener designed a multi-use retail, office, and residential building. The colours and neon signage of the neighbouring buildings are a nondescript patchwork within which the unadorned six-storey building stands out as a calm and solitary component. The facade is composed of sand-coloured reinforced concrete slabs, the same material and similar hue used by the architects for a museum addition in Biel and an embassy wing in Berlin. The changing rhythm in the window axes is a subtle gesture borrowed from conceptual art: it acts as a stimulating visual irritant in this central urban location. Two floors of retail shops are topped by offices and finally by a penthouse apartment under the flat roof. Records show that buildings have existed on this site even prior to the earthquake of 1356.

Architect:	Burckhardt+Partner AG, Dornacherstrasse 210, 4002 Basel
Client:	Canton Basel-Stadt, Department of civil services and environment, Planning department, Münsterplatz 11, 4001 Basel
Dates:	construction 1995–1998

LEONHARD HIGH SCHOOL

Leonhardsstrasse 15, 4051 Basel | Tram 3: Musik-Akademie | Tram 6 8 11 14 15 16: Barfüsserplatz

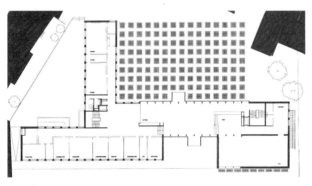

Ground floor

Architects Burckhardt Partner have expanded a city high school on Leonhardsstrasse by an addition of 13 000 square metres of floor space. The school complex consists of buildings from various eras, the earliest being 1884, then 1904–1906, 1957–1959, and the new addition. Together, these buildings represent a wide range of styles, from classical revival to Art Nouveau, post-war modern architecture, and New Objectivity. On a winding lot, the spatial requirements have been accommodated in an S-shaped building to which a long element was added. The complex has five upper storeys. A gym was installed underground, beneath the schoolyard. The previously dreary setting has been considerably improved with the new red-brown facade, the generously glazed, wind-sheltered entrance area off the piazza, and the planting of well-established trees.

View from entrance hall to schoolyard

Facade on schoolyard side with the "windows" of the underground gym

Architect:	Cruz/Ortiz Arquitectos, Santas Patronas 36, 41001 Seville, Spain,
	with Giraudi & Wettstein, Corso Pestalozzi 21b, 6900 Lugano
Client:	Schweizerische Bundesbahnen AG, Hochschulstrasse 6, 3000 Berne 65
	Canton Basel-Stadt, Department of civil services and environment,
	Planning department, Münsterplatz 11, 4001 Basel
Dates:	competition 1996, project planning 1996–2001, construction 2001–2003

PEDESTRIAN OVERPASS AT SBB TRAIN STATION

Centralbahnplatz/Güterstrasse, 4002 Basel | Tram 1 2 8 10 11 Bus 30 50: Centralbahnplatz | Tram 16: Güterstrasse

With a length of 184 metres, a width of 30 metres and a height of 15 metres, the pedestrian overpass of the SBB train station has been created as a free-spanning space, the airiness and brightness of which are unequalled in the city. The steel and glass structure is raised on a 8000 tonne foundation slab, which is covered in Norwegian quartzite slabs. Thirty-three escalators, a moving sidewalk and countless elevators guide the daily stream of users from this level into the station concourse. The architects from Seville (Cruz/Ortiz) and Lugano (Giraudi & Wettstein) have created a subtle division of the main terminal in the historic building by Faesch and la Roche (1904–07) and harmonized the rhythm of the new roof with the barrel vaults of the historic neighbouring structure. On the south side, the new structure projects dynamically into the Gundeldinger district. The project also created a new shopping promenade with 25 retail stores. A look at the Santa Justa train station in Seville (by Cruz/Ortiz 1988–91) reveals that the building masters from Spain and the Ticino have created a Mediterranean symbol.

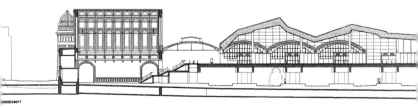

North-south section

G | BASEL: SUBURBS (EAST) AND GUNDELDINGEN

The 184-metre-long overpass

View from west

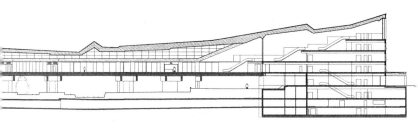

Architect:	Zwimpfer Partner, St. Alban-Anlage 66, 4002 Basel
Client:	Bauherrengemeinschaft Bahnhof Ost, Basel; PTT General Management, Berne; Immobiliengesellschaft Bahnhof Ost, Basel
Dates:	planning, projection,1986–1993 and construction 1994–2000

PETER MERIAN HOUSE

Peter Merian-Strasse 80–90 / Nauenstrasse, 4052 Basel | Tram 10 11: Peter Merian | Tram 1 2 8, Bus 30 50: Bahnhof SBB

Facade on Nauenstrasse   Site plan

At 180 metres in length, 60 metres in width, and 20 metres in height, the peter merian house is the largest administrative building to be constructed in the trinational urban area in the last twenty years. It was partially opened for use in 1999. The turquoise glass facade was developed by architects Zwimpfer Partner in collaboration with minimalist artist Donald Judd, who also contributed to the clear geometry of the overall form. The result is a building that resembles a monumental, serviceable, and artistic sculpture on this prominent site. The linear arrangement of six cubes and corresponding interior courtyards gives the building a serial structure. The atria, which rise through five floors, were designed by three women artists (Brigitte Kowanz, Ursula Mumenthaler, and Pipilotti Rist) and three male artists (François Morellet, Beat Zoderer, and Hans Danuser).

Courtyard with installation by Brigitte Kowanz

Architect:	Burckhardt + Partner AG, Dornacherstrasse 210, 4053 Basel
Client:	Winterthur Leben, General Guisan-Strasse 40, 8401 Winterthur
Dates:	competition 1999, construction 2001–2003

OFFICE AND HOUSING COMPLEX, THIERSTEINERALLEE

Thiersteinerallee 14–30, Tellstrasse 48–52, 60–66 | Tram 15 16: Heiliggeistkirche | Tram 10 11: Münchensteinerstrasse | Bus 36: Thiersteinerschule

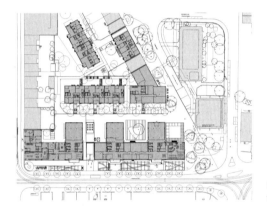

Site plan. In the foreground: the Thiersteinerallee

On a lot of barely 14 000 square metres, Burckhardt + Partner have erected a large office complex for a commercial enterprise and 69 apartments spread across five structures. A 130-metre-long, five-storey volume has been raised diagonally across from the new central switch-yard (project 51). Four large and nearly square glazed sections of 220 square metres each subdivide the monumental facade and redefine one of the most important street axis in the Gundeldinger district. The comb-like projection of the principal structure into a rear courtyard allows for optimal natural lighting and made it possible to reduce the overall building height. The resulting structure establishes correspondences to the neighbouring buildings from the late nineteenth and early twentieth century. The landscape architects Fahrni + Breitenfeld designed a verdant, publicly accessible garden.

BASEL: SUBURBS (EAST) AND GUNDELDINGEN

Facade overlooking the Münchensteinerbrücke

The building slabs in the courtyard

Facade seen from the Heiliggeistkirche

Architect:	Diener & Diener, Henric Petri-Strasse 22, 4010 Basel
Client:	Swiss Bank Association, Basel
Dates:	construction 1990–1994

UBS TRAINING AND CONFERENCE CENTRE

Viaduktstrasse 33, 4052 Basel | Tram 1 2 8 16: Markthalle | Tram 6 10: Heuwaage

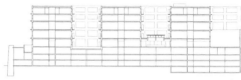

Aerial view of complex from the east

East-west section

The three-wing complex on Viaduktstrasse

The training and conference centre of the UBS (formerly Swiss Bank Association), designed by Diener & Diener, together with the new building by Richard Meier (project 22, on the opposite side of the street), accentuates the east wing of the Swiss and French railway station in Basel. The architects composed the large complex (56 000 m²) out of long blocks in an orthogonal arrangement along a curve. Thanks to windows facing east, south, and west, the offices and lecture halls receive maximum natural light, while the facade on the busy main street is almost windowless. An underground car park is easily accessible at ground level behind a massive wall set into the hillside. In the near future, a new track for the Basel-Paris line will run parallel to the curved rear wall of the conference centre.

BASEL: BACHLETTEN AND BRUDERHOLZ, BINNINGEN, BOTTMINGEN, MÜNCHENSTEIN

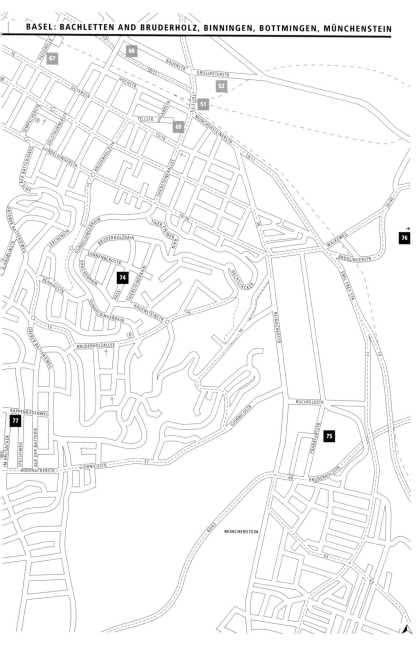

Architect:	Wymann & Selva, Basel
	Since 1997 Luca Selva, Viaduktstrasse 14, 4051 Basel
	and Jean-Pierre Wymann, Viaduktstrasse 14, 4051 Basel
	Associates Hans Gritsch, Stefan Segessenmann
Client:	Canton Basel-Stadt, Department of civil services and environment,
	Planning department, Münsterplatz 11, 4001 Basel
Dates:	competition 1993/1994, construction 1995–1996

KALTBRUNNEN SCHOOLHOUSE

Kaltbrunnen-Promenade 95, 4054 Basel | Tram 8: Laupenring | Bus 36: Holee

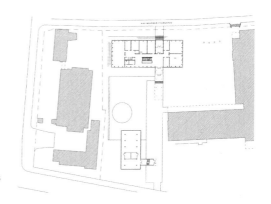

Site plan: to the left, Herman Baur's
All Saints Church

Next to the original Neubad Schoolhouse – a late 1940s complex desined by Giovanni Panozzo – Wymann & Selva have created the new Kaltbrunnen Schoolhouse, thereby more than doubling the size of the school complex. The new structure has a historic neighbour in Hermann Baur's All Saints Church (1948–1950). The architects consciously sought to avoid a stylistic clash; instead, they structured the open space, created differentiated building heights, and preserved the mature trees on the site. Located above a low-lying track of the Basel-France line, the exposed site allowed for fully glazed facades on all sides of the new four-storey main building. The concrete floors which project through the facades create an elegant visual rhythm. Christoph Rösch's "Sound Cylinder" could be described as a land-art object for this complex.

The light cube of the auditorium

Facade on low-lying railway track

Architect:	Hanspeter Müller, St. Johanns-Vorstadt 3, 4056 Basel
Client:	Binningen community association, Curt Goetz-Strasse 1, 4102 Binningen
Dates:	project planning 1994, construction 1995

YOUTH CENTRE

In den Schutzmatten 10, 4102 Binningen | Tram 2, Bus 34: Hohle Gasse | Tram 10 17: Binningen Oberdorf

Facade overlooking the Birsig River

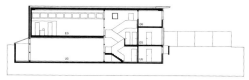

East-west section

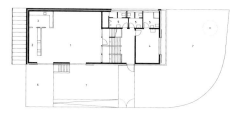

Ground-floor plan

Hanspeter Müller designed a new youth centre in Binningen. The structure on Baslerstrasse is located next to a small tributary of the Rhine (the Birsig), in a green yet urban location with excellent access to public transportation. Large communal rooms (café, disco) and an equally spacious patio provide a well-considered physical environment for the varied and largely self-directed leisure activities of young people. The beautiful location is complemented by an architecture that appreciates the surrounding elements: this applies both to the sensitive choice of building materials and to the generous design of the interior and exterior spaces.

Architect:	Peter Stiner, Clarastrasse 7, 4058 Basel
Landscape design:	August Künzel, Oslostrasse 5, 4053 Basel
	Execution: Martin Rauch, Schlins, Austria
Client:	Zoological Gardens, Binningerstrasse 40, 4054 Basel
	Project management: Thomas Schönbächler
Dates:	construction 1998–2003

ETOSCHA HOUSE IN THE ZOOLOGICAL GARDENS

Binningerstrasse 40, 4054 Basel | Tram 10: Zoo | Tram 2, Bus 34 36: Zoo Dorenbach | Tram 6 16: Heuwaage

South elevation

Etoscha is a strip of land with a national park in Namibia. The new pavilion for predators in the Zoological Gardens, which were opened in 1874, was named after this region. The architecture follows a philosophy that aims for a spatial continuum for grown nature (garden) and built nature (architecture). In this setting, buildings cannot enter the scene as confident gestures; instead they serve as subordinate elements in the overall form. The winding path through the polygon (roughly 35 by 32 metres in area) combines experiential space with an environment that is compatible for the featured fauna and flora. The slanted, fan-shaped position of the windows renders them invisible to the visitor, suggesting a feeling of being under the open skies. A panorama window at the entrance offers a link between the climate requirements of this region (air temperature/humidity, flora) and the re-created landscape of the outdoor enclosure. The rammed-earth walls are a reference to the aesthetics of building styles and materials in South-western Africa.

BASEL: BACHLETTEN AND BRUDERHOLZ, BINNINGEN, BOTTMINGEN, MÜNCHENSTEIN

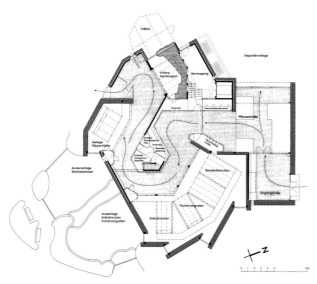

Ground plan

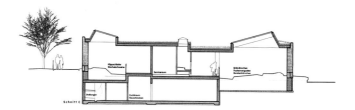

West-east section

Architect:	Silvia Gmür, Pfluggässlein 3, 4001 Basel
Client:	F. Steiner, Basel
Dates:	construction 1990

ONE-ROOM HOUSE

Sonnenbergstrasse 92, 4059 Basel | Tram 15: Wolfschlucht | Tram 16: Hauensteinstrasse

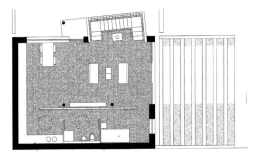

Ground floor

The Bruderholz neighbourhood was developed in the twentieth century and has few interesting architectural features. Some individual houses and row houses were co-operative projects. Many villas were constructed on large lots, and it is to this circumstance that Silvia Gmür's new building owes its existence: it occupies the space previously used for garages. The narrow structure on a concrete base, a single storey in steel and wood construction, is topped by a shallow gable roof. A kind of portico is set at a slight angle to the entrance facade. Two-thirds of the portico wall is glass brick, with the unfenestrated remainder providing a monumental frame around the front door. The glass-brick wall has the character of a very large minimalist picture that is transformed into a light sculpture when lit at night.

The portico on Sonnenbergstrasse

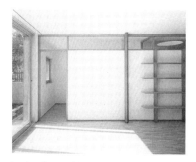

Interior with view of the garden

Architekt:	Herzog & de Meuron, Rheinschanze 6, 4056 Basel
Bauherr:	Laurenz-Stiftung, Ruchfeldstrasse 19, 4142 Münchenstein/Basel
Termine:	Projekt 1998–1999, Ausführung 2000–2003

SCHAULAGER OF THE LAURENZ FOUNDATION

Ruchfeldstrasse 19, 4141 Münchenstein | Tram 11, Bus 60: Schaulager | Bus 36: Dreispitz

West facade with a composite of excavation pebble and concrete

With an area of 16 500 square metres on five floors, the exhibition warehouse of the Laurenz Foundation in the industrial district of Münchenstein is a building that presents a hermetically closed exterior and reveals its qualities in the interior. The exhibition areas (basement and ground floor, 3 350 m^2) and the storage areas (floors 2 to 4, 7 500 m^2) house the roughly 650 works of art of the Emanuel Hoffmann Foundation and are arranged around a 28-metre-high atrium. Virtual windows in the form of LED screens are incorporated into the entrance facade, wich is compressed into a trapezoid shape. Works from the collection are displayed in large-scale and monumental formats on these screens. The untreated oak floor in the basement and on the ground floor invests the building with the ambience of a luxury loft. The auditorium with 144 purple arm chairs, walls and ceiling covered in carefully worked metal screens and a picture window set into the face wall has the feeling of a sanctuary. The exhibition warehouse is only open to the public from May to September.

The 28-metre-high atrium

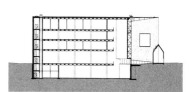

West-east section

Floor plan of 2nd to 4th floor

Architect:	Berrel Architekten, Missionsstrasse 35a, 4055 Basel with
	Zwimpfer Partner Krarup Furrer, St. Alban-Anlage 66, 4052 Basel
Client:	Genossenschaft Regionale Eissporthalle St. Jakob, Hölzlistrasse 36, 4102 Binningen
Dates:	project planning and construction 2001–2002

ST. JAKOBARENA

Brüglingen 33, 4142 Münchenstein | Tram 14, Bus 36: St. Jakob

Facade with main entrance

The facade is the dress for the new skating rink: the architects have stretched 30 textile squares, each roughly 80 square metres (8.9 by 9.7 metres), in front of the concrete oval foundation and their elegant steel-and-glass structure. The more than 100-metre-long and roughly 20-metre-high building, which can accommodate 6 000 spectators, lies in the plain of St. Jakob like a monochromatic film strip. The site can look back on a long history of international sporting events. The arena features an innovative heating- and ventilation system, opening new doors in terms of ecological and economic operation. A filigree metal construction allows for a column-free 70-metre-wide interior. The zinc of the metal banisters and night-blue seats create an ambience of temporary and tranquil comfort. The usage programme is rounded out with facilities for intramurals and private sports clubs.

BASEL: BACHLETTEN AND BRUDERHOLZ, BINNINGEN, BOTTMINGEN, MÜNCHENSTEIN

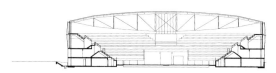

South-north section

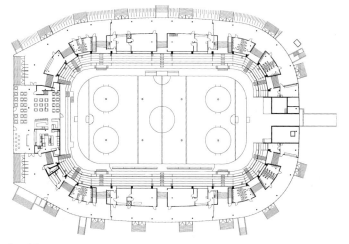

Ground plan

Architect:	Herzog & de Meuron, Rheinschanze 6, 4056 Basel
	Project management Renée Levy
Client:	E. Brunner-Sulzer, Bottmingen
Dates:	project planning 1984, construction 1985

PLYWOOD HOUSE

Rappenbodenweg 6, 4103 Bottmingen | Bus 37 63: Bruderholzspital | Tram 15: Studio Basel

The bend in the facade, designed to accommodate the Paulownia imperialis

Rhythmic arrangement of windows
on the south side

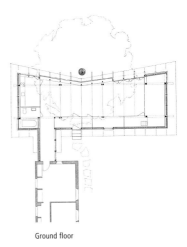

Ground floor

The villa expansion came to be called the Plywood House because of the material used in the facade, while its shape was determined by the presence of a large tree on the site. To accommodate the tree, a Paulownia imperialis, architects Herzog & de Meuron slightly angled one side of the rectangular plan, creating an inward fold along one facade. The gently sloped gable roof extends into a generous overhang on all sides. Elevated on low supports, the structure has a lightness reminiscent of Japanese pavilions. The facade is divided into a grid of equal squares. The forty-two squares on the angled south side allow for playful treatment of windows: a ribbon of windows on one side, a panoramic window stretching the full height in the centre, and clerestory windows above.

Architect:	Michael Alder, St. Alban-Vorstadt 24, 4052 Basel
	Associate Roland Naegelin; now Atelier Gemeinschaft,
	St. Johanns-Vorstadt 3, 4056 Basel
Clients:	D. and M. Reicke, Bottmingen
Dates:	project planning 1987, construction 1988

SINGLE-FAMILY HOUSE

Kirschbaumweg 27, 4103 Bottmingen | Bus 61: Bertschenacker | Bus 34: Blauenstrasse

The facade overlooking the garden

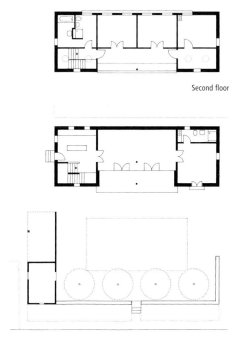

Second floor

Ground floor and garden

It is rare for a single-family house to be designed around its central axes. Yet Michael Alder's layout for the house in Bottmingen is centred on both the longitudinal axis and the transverse axis. The entrance on the narrow west side leads straight into the living space. At the far wall of the adjoining room the corridor ends in a square window. The living room has a fully glazed wall looking onto the garden – a band of light that recurs on the upper floor in the hallway leading to the bedroom and library wing. The balanced harmony of the interior carries over to the exterior. With its fine wood siding, the facade exudes an air of contemplative stillness and confident containment.

Architect:	Ackermann & Friedli, Schützenmattstrasse 43, 4051 Basel
	Since 1999 Ackermann Architekt
Client:	Community Living Foundation, Bottmingen
Dates:	competition 1994, project planning 1996/1997, construction 1998–1999

AM BIRSIG COMMUNITY CENTRE AND HOUSING

Löchlimattstrasse 6, 4103 Bottmingen | Tram 10 17: Stallen

Ground floor

On a quiet lot bordering the Birsig River and located slightly below a main artery road, Ackermann & Friedli have created a centre for community activities and community living. These separate uses are served by two individual structures whose main entrances face each other beneath a connecting roof. The residential unit has direct access to outdoor patios; the upper floor features operable skylights. These brick-faced buildings are animated by large windows, carefully selected wood and stone floors, and spacious entrance areas. Exterior views and interior perspectives are varied, creating a stimulating yet contemplative atmosphere.

Facade overlooking the Birsig River

Terrace on upper floor with wall openings

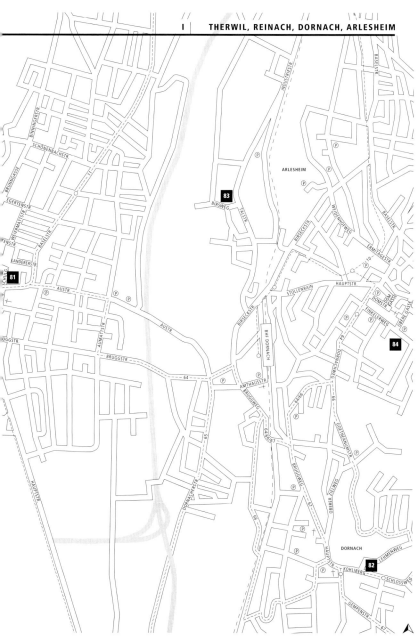

Architect:	Herzog & de Meuron, Rheinschanze 6, 4056 Basel
	Project management Annette Gigon
Clients:	H. and M. Vögtlin-König, Therwil
Dates:	project planning 1985, construction 1986

HOUSE FOR AN ART COLLECTOR

Lerchenrainstrasse 5, 4106 Therwil | Tram 10 17: Känelmatt | Bus 64: Jurastrasse

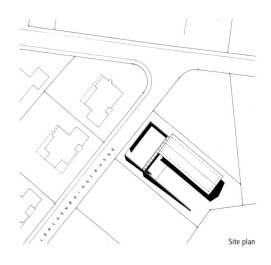

Site plan

The house for an art collector in Therwil is a single-family home with an exhibition space. The general orientation is similar to the Courtyard Residential Building (see project 8). The hermetic character of the building was perceived as provocative for some time in this rural town environment south of the city, perhaps owing to its uncompromising use of exposed concrete. With its introverted air and gravelled courtyard, the building makes clear reference to Tadao Ando's Japanese residential designs. The structure is oriented along the length of the deep lot. The lot extends slightly at the south-west end, making it hexagonal, which provides some rhythm in the design without disturbing its confident air of equanimity.

Section

Enclosed environment

The gravelled courtyard

Architect:	Morger & Degelo, Spitalstrasse 8, 4056 Basel
Client:	Community of Reinach, Hauptstrasse 10, 4153 Reinach
Dates:	competition 1997, project planning and construction 1998–2002

COMMUNITY CENTRE REINACH

Hauptstrasse 10, 4153 Reinach | Tram 11: Landererstrasse | Bus 64: Reinach Dorf

Facade on the main street

The goal was to achieve a presence with a building in Reinach comparable to that of similar public buildings in the old cities of northern Italy. This is precisely what Morger & Degelo succeeded in creating with a nearly square cube for the community administration. The four-storey glass block is the core of an ensemble that also contains apartment and commercial buildings. For the first time since 1964, the administration of the community is once again housed under one roof. In the interior of the "palazzo pubblico," an open gallery court directly behind the main entrance provides centralized access. The floor covering in Greek marble is both refined and hardwearing. Between the second and the fourth floor, where the corridors and window axes of the building rotate windmill-like by 90 degrees each, windows stretching across the entire height and width of the rooms offer twelve different picture postcard views. The space in front of the main street elevation has been gently terraced and has become a piazza for Reinach.

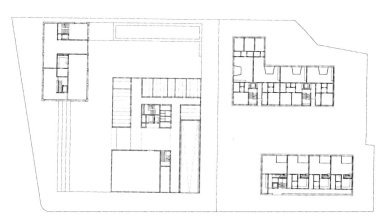

The four buildings of the ensemble
with the main street (left)

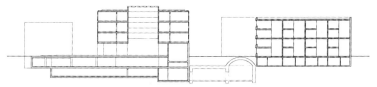

South-north section

Architect:	Morger & Degelo, Spitalstrasse 8, 4056 Basel
	Associate Nadja Keller
Clients:	A. and Ch. Nadolny, Dornach
Dates:	project planning and construction 1995–1996

SINGLE-FAMILY HOUSE

Lehmenweg 2/Schlossweg, 4143 Dornach | Bus 66: Quidum | Bus 67: Museumsplatz

South facade

Second floor

Ground floor

Architects Morger & Degelo built a single-family house in Dornach on the southern edge of metropolitan Basel, within walking distance of Rudolf Steiner's famous Goetheanum. The severe design – the unbroken cedar facade to the north gives the house a box-like appearance – echoes the traditional wooden farmhouses of the area, some of which are preserved in the village of Dornach. The two floors contain a total of 200 square metres of living space. Generously proportioned windows to the south, east, and west open the sophisticated wood structure to landscape and light. The public area (living room, etc.) and the private area (bedrooms, etc.) are set apart by the use of different materials: slate for the ground floor and parquet flooring upstairs. Two right angles are joined to form a slightly trapezoidal ground plan.

Architect:	Proplaning, Burgfelderstrasse 211, 4025 Basel
Client:	Baselland civic servants pension fund, Liestal;
	Basel civic servants pension fund, Basel
Dates:	construction 1997–1999

OBERE WIDEN RESIDENTIAL DEVELOPMENT

Birseckstrasse/Talstrasse, 4144 Arlesheim | Tram 10: Stollenrain | Train, Bus 64 65 66 67: Dornach Bahnhof

One of five long buildings with clinker-brick facades

The row houses in wood construction

THERWIL, REINACH, DORNACH, ARLESHEIM

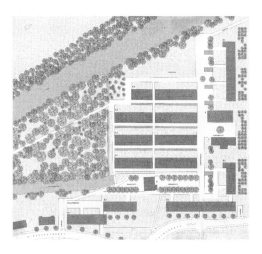

Site plan: the clinker-faced buildings frame the wooden row houses in the centre

Proplaning designed a new residential complex in the town of Arlesheim on a 4.2 hectare lot that includes an 8000-square-metre nature preserve along the Birs, a tributary of the Rhine. Five powerful clinker-brick buildings, up to 100 metres long, line the site of a former textile factory. The architects placed forty wooden row houses into the factory court in four parallel rows that follow the lines of the former factory shed roofs. The houses are structured in the fashion of maisonette apartments, with attic rooms on the roof with large dormer windows. In the horizontal extension, the windows emulate the window ribbons of early industrial architecture. The 180 apartments, with up to five rooms per unit, set an urban accent in this area of suburban sprawl to the south-east of Basel.

Architect:	Klaus Schuldt, Rittergasse 29, 4051 Basel and Andreas Scheiwiller, since 1999
	Dolenc Scheiwiller Architekten, St. Jakobs-Strasse 54, 4052 Basel
	Associates Carmen Müller, Thomas Grasser
Client:	Dorenbach AG, Basel; P. and S. Dudler, H.P. von Hahn, N. and L. Hosch,
	J. C. Müller, K. and G. Schuldt, Arlesheim
Dates:	Project planning 1996, construction 1997–2000

ZUM WISSE SEGEL, VILLAS

Zum wisse Segel 5, 7, 10, 11, 12, 4144 Arlesheim | Bus 64: Bromhübel | Tram 10: Arlesheim Dorf

Site plan with ground-floor plans

Architects Klaus Schuldt and Andreas Scheiwiller designed five two-storey detached homes ranging from 240 to 300 square metres in ground plan for a barely 5400-square-metre lot in Arlesheim. Despite the rural environment, the homes have an urban character by virtue of their precise arrangement and their proximity to the cathedral square. The Baroque ensemble and the cathedral itself, together with four massive residential and administration buildings, were the first major architecture outside the southern boundary of Basel. In the new development, the architects have structured the houses with floor-to-ceiling glass fronts, opening them to light and to the gardens. The designs deliberately reflect typologies developed by Mies van der Rohe in the 1920s (Wolf House in Guben, 1925–1926 and Lange House in Krefeld, 1928).

Northwest elevation of House 10 and House 12

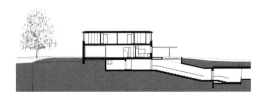

Longitudinal section of House 11

Architect:	François Fasnacht, Spalenvorstadt 8, 4003 Basel
Client:	Balimpex AG, Frohburgerstrasse 21, 4132 Muttenz
Dates:	project planning 1995, construction 1995–1996

OFFICE BUILDING WITH PENTHOUSE APARTMENT

Frohburgerstrasse 21, 4132 Muttenz | Train: Muttenz Bahnhof | Tram 14, Bus 60: Muttenz Dorf

Courtyard facade with penthouse

To the east, the city disintegrates into unchecked residential, commercial, and industrial sprawl. François Fasnacht has created a symbol of calmness and concentration with a three-storey structure in Muttenz. Access to the two office floors is provided from a vestibule that has been set into the main structure. The building's most striking element is a large window onto which the company name has been affixed in tall, narrow capital letters. When work continues into the night, this creates an urban display window visible from the street. The apartment with roof patio has a separate entrance from the ground floor. A monochromatic yellow painting by Hans Sieverding hangs in the two-storey reception area.

The large window with adjoining vestibule

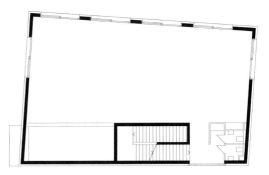

Ground floor

Architect:	Bürgin Nissen Wentzlaff, St. Alban-Vorstadt 80, 4052 Basel
	Since 2001 Nissen & Wentzlaff Architekten
Client:	Coop Basel Liestal Fricktal, Güterstrasse 190, 4053 Basel
Dates:	project planning 1995, construction 1996–1998

HOTEL, SUPERMARKET, APARTMENTS

St. Jakobs-Strasse 1/Hauptstrasse, 4132 Muttenz | Train: Muttenz Bahnhof | Tram 14, Bus 60: Muttenz Dorf

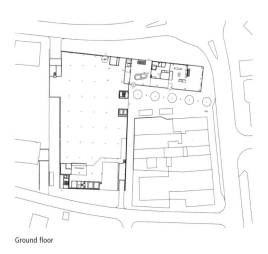

Ground floor

Architects Bürgin Nissen Wentzlaff designed a supermarket with 2500 square metres of floor space, a 200-bed hotel, and apartments in the town of Muttenz for their client, the Swiss grocery chain Coop. The fully glazed base was placed onto the L-shaped lot, and two tall structures rise from this base. The one-flight staircase, accessing the five floors and the hotel, is the most noticeable design element of the complex. On the south side of the supermarket, five maisonette apartments were built, which can be reached by a covered walkway. The facade with vertical glazed rectangles and perforated white aluminium shutters is a showcase feature.

The single-flight staircase across five floors

Architect:	Frank O. Gehry + Associates, 1520B Cloverfield Boulevard,
	Santa Monica, California 90404 USA
	Project management, planning and site management Günter Pfeifer,
	Industriestrasse 2, 79541 Lörrach, in partnership with Roland Mayer
Client:	Vitrashop AG, Klünenfeldstrasse 22, 4127 Birsfelden
Dates:	construction 1992–1994

VITRA-CENTER
Klünenfeldstrasse 22, 4127 Birsfelden | Tram 3: Birsfelden Hard

The deconstructivist architecture
of the Villa

J | MUTTENZ, BIRSFELDEN

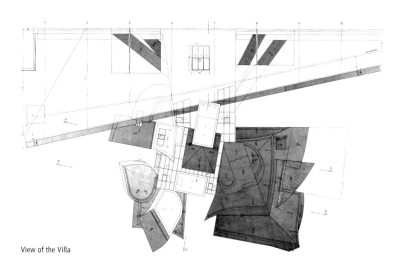

View of the Villa

Frank O. Gehry's first building in Switzerland – and Vitra's second home – was opened in Birsfelden in 1994 (see also project 104, Gehry's first building in Europe). The office wing responds to the existing Vitra building from 1957, whose facade is similarly structured. For the "Villa", which houses the reception rooms and serves as the main entrance to the company's head office, Gehry has delved into the treasure chest of his imagination for a playful combination of spherical, convex, concave, and other geometric shapes. These expressive forms are covered in titanium cladding; large lighting fixtures are prototypes; individual rooms are painted in pop colours. Some sections of the 6000-square-metre structure seem like a designer's adventure playground.

Architect:	Bürgin Nissen Wentzlaff, St. Alban-Vorstadt 80, 4052 Basel
	Since 2001 Nissen & Wentzlaff Architekten
Client:	main building: Cantonal Bank of Baselland, Liestal;
	annex building: P. Leuenberger, Birsfelden
Dates:	project planning 1993, construction 1994–1996

BANK AND OFFICE BUILDING

Hauptstrasse 75/77, 4127 Birsfelden | Tram 3: Schulstrasse

The austere south facade

In Birsfelden the Cantonal Bank of Baselland commissioned a new office building complete with retail shops and office areas for its subsidiary. Architects Bürgin Nissen Wentzlaff were faced with a challenging site and designed a building that presents two very different faces. Its concept is both classically modern and anarchic. Two facades meet at a ninety-degree angle in a clash of contrasting materials (white stone, blue glass) and different design philosophies. The vertical windows on two sides are asynchronously arranged and the horizontal window ribbon makes one think of a jazz score. Nevertheless, this is a measured, "metric" architecture that follows an additive order. It creates a lyrical anchor for the "loud" urban site.

J | **MUTTENZ, BIRSFELDEN**

The melodic north facade

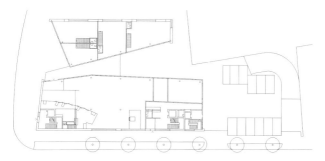

Ground floor

Architect:	Rolf Brüderlin, Bachgässlein 6, 4125 Riehen
	Associates Alex Callierotti, Giuseppe Pontillo
Client:	Canton Basel-Stadt, Department of civil services and environment,
	Planning department, Münsterplatz 11, 4001 Basel
Dates:	construction 1993–1994

HEBEL SCHOOL EXPANSION

Langenlängeweg 14, 4125 Riehen | Bus 31 34 45: Rauracher | Tram 6: Niederholz

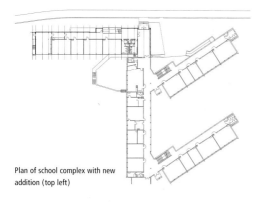

Plan of school complex with new addition (top left)

Rolf Brüderlin added a long block onto an existing school complex designed by Tibère Vadi (completed in 1951) in Riehen. Since the site was previously occupied by a kindergarten in wood construction designed by Hans Bernoulli (1945) – a structure much liked by students, teachers, and local residents – the architect decided to employ the same skin on the street facade. The reddish brown louvred facade functions as an element of visual archaeology. The south and garden facades are kept a delicate yellow. Brüderlin has established a link to the original building by means of a mirror image: the glass stairwell. Vadi made the stairs visible from the outside through a two-storey glass rectangle. A few metres farther along, there now exists an almost exact duplicate.

The stairs at the two-storey-high windows

Architect:	Metron AG, Stahlrain 2, 5201 Brugg
	Markus Gasser, Urs Deppeler, Heini Glauser
	Supervision Brogli + Müller, Basel
Client:	Wohnstadt Bau- und Verwaltungs-Genossenschaft Basel,
	Viaduktstrasse 12, 4051 Basel
Dates:	project planning 1990/1991, construction 1992–1994

IM NIEDERHOLZBODEN HOUSING DEVELOPMENT

Im Niederholzboden/Arnikastrasse 12–26, 4125 Riehen | Tram 6: Niederholz

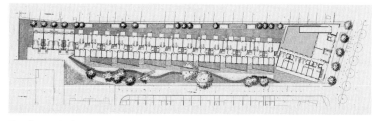

Plan of housing development

With a length of 200 metres, the Niederholzboden housing development lies like an anchor in heavily parcelled south Riehen. A main building with twelve apartments and two communal rooms is followed by another two-storey block that accommodates thirty apartments and four row houses. Metron Architekten were able to generate considerable energy savings for heating and ventilation, making this an energy-efficient development. Large balconies and a facade of yellow and red-brown wood panels define the look of the flat-roofed buildings, which enjoy a considerable depth of 14 metres. In den Habermatten (1924–1926) – a development that was equally trend-setting for its time – lies nearby.

Aerial view of the compact scheme

Main building with common rooms

Architect:	Rolf Furrer und François Fasnacht, Basel
	Since 1995 Rolf Furrer, St. Johanns-Vorstadt 38, 4056 Basel
	and François Fasnacht, Spalenvorstadt 8, 4051 Basel
Client:	Basel Transport Services, Basel;
	Community of Riehen, Riehen
Dates:	project planning and construction 1992 and 1994–1995

RIEHEN DORF TRAM SHELTER
Baselstrasse | Tram 6: Riehen Dorf

LACHENWEG BUS SHELTER
Lachenweg/Grenzacherweg | Bus 34 45: Lachenweg

A competition in 1985 helped to create a new look for Basel's 230 tram and bus shelters. Two standard types for tram and bus shelters were established. The first has a rectangular plan which can be adapted to local topography in depth and width; and the second is a round, rain-protected shelter with seating, intended mostly for residential neighbourhoods. The elliptical shape of the stop in the village of Riehen is a prototype. The elegant structure designed by Rolf Furrer and François Fasnacht (since 1996 Furrer has managed the project on his own) creates a focal point for the Riehen streetscape. The small structure is characterized by glass walls in a stacked arrangement and a skylight.

Section and plan of the tram shelter
Riehen-Dorf

The elliptical construction

The bus shelter Lachenweg:
front view, plan, and section

Architect:	Stump & Schibli Architekten, Elisabethenstrasse 28, 4051 Basel
Client:	Canton Basel-Stadt, Department of civil services and environment,
	Planning department, Münsterplatz 11, 4001 Basel
Dates:	competition 1995, construction 2000–2004 (3rd stage 2004–2005)

"ZUR HOFFNUNG" – RESIDENTIAL SCHOOL FOR CHILDREN

Wenkenstrasse 33, 4125 Riehen | Tram 6: Bettingerstr. | Bus 32: Martinsrain | Bus 34: Bahnübergang | S6: Riehen-Bahnhof

View from basement level
into courtyard

One of the facades overlooking
the Wenkenstrasse

Site plan

On the eastern slope overlooking the old town core of Riehen, Stump & Schibli have transformed the "Zur Hoffnung" school into a small residential and training centre for children with disabilities. Two massive stone buildings (both circa 1900) have been preserved from the historic ensemble on the nearly 29 000 square metre lot. Thus far, six new buildings (including two agricultural buildings) have been added to form the new complex. A therapy building is still under construction. Three residential- and communal buildings have been set into the slope in such a clever manner as to appear like large private residences with their generous windows and clear outlines. Concrete, brick coping, parquet flooring and a sensual as well as efficient lighting scheme generate an atmosphere of warm and elegant objectivity. The visual links between all of the volumes create a spatial cohesion within the park-like setting.

Architect:	Renzo Piano, 34, rue des Archives, F-75004 Paris
	Management Burckhardt Partner, Basel
Client:	Beyeler Foundation, Baselstrasse 77, 4125 Riehen
Dates:	project planning 1992, construction 1994–1997, expansion 2000

BEYELER FOUNDATION MUSEUM

Baselstrasse 101, 4125 Riehen | Tram 6: Fondation Beyeler | Bus 16 ÜL3: Weilstrasse

Ground floor

For the art collection of the Beyeler Foundation, Renzo Piano has created an elegant museum suffused with light. The approximately 3000-square-metre exhibition area is spread across two floors in a 125-metre-long building. Slightly lowered into the ground, the delicate structure is only visible in its entirety from a river plain behind the building. Since the administration and museum restaurant are located in a Baroque-style house, the architect was free to build a museum that represents an ideal within this typology. This work joins the ranks of famous museums worldwide, such as those designed by Henry van de Velde (Otterloo), Jørgen Bo and Vilhelm Wohlert (Zeeland), Frank Lloyd Wright (New York), Ludwig Mies van der Rohe (Berlin), and Louis I. Kahn (Fort Worth).

The museum and the park

Architect:	Wilfrid and Katharina Steib, Unterer Rheinweg 56, 4057 Basel
Client:	Ecumenical Foundation, Wendelin House Nursing Home, Riehen
Dates:	competition 1985, construction 1986–1988

HAUS ZUM WENDELIN NURSING HOME

Inzlingerstrasse 50, 4125 Riehen | Bus 32 ÜL3: Hinter Gärten | Tram 6, Bus 16: Weilstrasse

Facades on garden side

Facade on Inzlingerstrasse

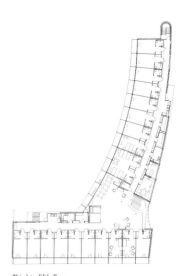

Third to fifth floor

The Wendelin House nursing home in Riehen follows the street in a gentle curve. The south facade on the garden side of the four-storey, L-shaped building describes a dynamic, outward-reaching curve. Wilfrid and Katharina Steib's design on this side is almost fully glazed, with balconies formed by covered walkways that run the length of each floor. The administration offices and communal rooms are on the ground floor. The entrance to this area lies on the fully glazed garden side, and these rooms are thus suffused with light. The predominant colours are pastel shades. Notable architectural projects (projects 93 and 95) have been realized to the north and west, almost in the same neighbourhood.

Architect:	Michael Alder, St. Alban-Vorstadt 24, 4052 Basel
	Associate Roland Naegelin; now Atelier Gemeinschaft,
	St. Johanns-Vorstadt 3, 4056 Basel
Client:	HERA and Kettenacker housing cooperative, Riehen
Dates:	competition 1989, construction 1991–1992

VOGELBACH HOUSING DEVELOPMENT

Friedhofweg 30–80, 4125 Riehen | Tram 6, Bus 16 ÜL3: Weilstrasse

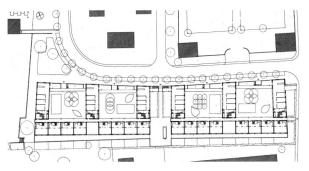

Plan of the 200-metre-long complex

Close to the German border, Michael Alder designed the Vogelbach housing co-op in Riehen. The complex contains forty single-level and duplex apartments, ranging from bachelor to five rooms. Since the 1920s, Riehen has been the site of many cooperative building projects. Paul Artaria, Hans Schmidt, and Hans Bernoulli, three pioneers of the New Architecture, have left their imprint in this district. Michael Alder continued the tradition: he grouped the differentiated cubical volumes around courtyards, arranging balconies, patios, and all exterior spaces along the south side for maximum sun exposure. Alder's design is deliberately urban by comparison to Hans Schmidt's more rural development from the post-war period.

Facade on Friedhofweg

One of five courtyards

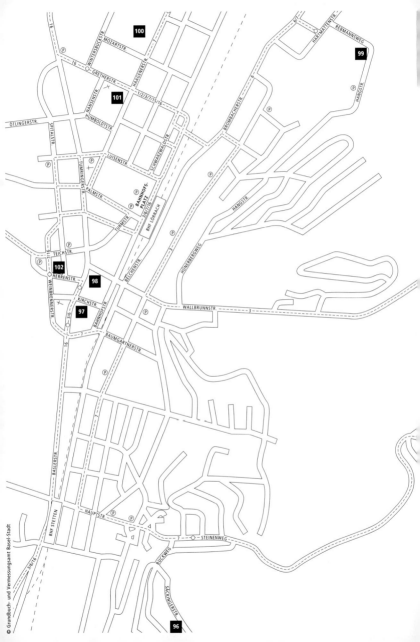

L | LÖRRACH

Architect:	Günter Pfeifer, Industriestrasse 2, D-79541 Lörrach
	in partnership with Roland Mayer
Client:	H. Lorenz, Lörrach
Dates:	construction 1992

SINGLE-FAMILY HOUSE

Säckingerstrasse 26, D-79540 Lörrach | Bus 7: Steinenweg | Train, Bus ÜL3 3 6 16: Stetten Bahnhof

South-west facade

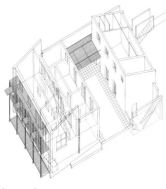

Axonometric

View towards France and Switzerland

Günter Pfeifer has constructed a single-family house on the Dinkelberg hillside with views to the south and south-east. The design consists of two elongated, parallel buildings. Shed roofs to the street and on the valley side create a contained, enclosed complex. To the north-west, an 18-metre wall separates the building from its neighbour; an integrated louvred section allows light to pass through the wall. The floor plans are based on Euclidian geometries. Wherever possible, glass skins stretch from floor to ceiling, creating shafts of light and sightlines deep into the building. Access from the street is provided via steps down to the ground floor and a wooden footbridge to the upper floor.

Architect:	Günter Pfeifer, Industriestrasse 2, D-79541 Lörrach
	in partnership with Roland Mayer
Client:	City of Lörrach, Stadtbauamt, Luisenstrasse 16, D-79537 Lörrach
Dates:	construction 1992–1993

DEPARTMENT STORE CONVERSION INTO LIBRARY

Baslerstrasse 128, D-79539 Lörrach | Bus ÜL3 3 6 7 16: Museum | Train: Lörrach Bahnhof

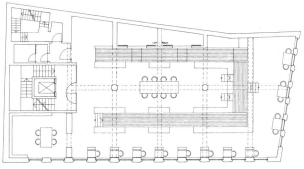

Third floor

A department store from circa 1900 was converted by Günter Pfeifer into Lörrach's public library. The four-storey structure with windows on two sides now includes an open-plan library, well-lit study areas, and a play area in the children's and youth section. The auditorium in the basement is reserved for lectures and other events. The architect has surrounded two load-bearing columns in the entrance area with four symmetrically arranged round metal pieces in a matt finish, connecting them by means of an elliptical polished rail into a sculptural unit. This creates an acoustic and visual barrier between the lending and the reading areas, and also serves as an exhibition space for new library acquisitions.

View into reading area

Architect:	Schaudt Architekten, Hafenstrasse 10, D-78462 Konstanz
Client:	Verlagshaus Oberbadisches Volksblatt with Sparkasse Lörrach and ÖVA Mannheim
Dates:	competition 1992, project planning and construction 1993–1996

ALT STAZIONE CINEMA CAFÉ

Baslerstrasse 164/166, D-79539 Lörrach | Bus ÜL3 3 6 7 16: Alter Markt | Train: Lörrach Bahnhof

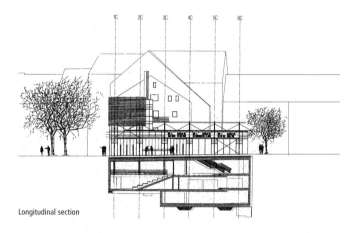

Longitudinal section

In the 1990s the Alter Markt neighbourhood was extensively refurbished and several new buildings were erected in the area. The most decisive intervention occurred with the construction of a slender steel and glass building designed by Schaudt Architekten. A mere 4 metres in width, more than 20 metres long, and approximately 10 metres high, it accommodates a café and three cinemas located underground. Miniature in its built environment, the structure nevertheless has an air of autonomy and urbanity because it doesn't seek to compete visually with any of the surrounding architecture. It is constructed on a modular grid and exudes the confident air of a free-standing building, even though it was simply added on to a four-storey office and residential building. The fire wall remains unchanged, with the exception of a new surface treatment.

Facade on Baslerstrasse

Architect:	Detlef Würkert and Hans Ueli Felchlin, Feldbergstrasse 1, D-79539 Lörrach
Client:	Städtische Wohnbaugesellschaft Lörrach, Schillerstrasse 4, D-79540 Lörrach
Dates:	project planning and construction 1995–1998

HOUSING DEVELOPMENT

Hangstrasse / Rebmannsweg, D-79539 Lörrach | Bus 6 7: Rebmannsweg

Floor plan of a row house

Detlef Würkert and Hans Ueli Felchlin built terraced housing and multi-generational apartments in the north-east of the city. The two three-storey, 60-metre-long buildings (a third is under construction) contain six two-room, twelve three-room, and twelve five-room units. Bands of windows and a louvred wood facade are visible from the valley. Wooden folding and sliding shutters underline the "Japanese" character of the complex. From the hillside road the buildings are accessed across a sunken courtyard. The maisonette apartments in the second building can be combined with the units on the ground floor. Attention to detail in the planning makes this development comparable to social housing developments in Riehen (project 95) and Basel (project 29).

L | LÖRRACH

The two long buildings seen from Rebmannsweg

Window in one of the eat-in kitchens

Architect:	Wilhelm + Partner, Am Unteren Sonnenrain 4, D-79539 Lörrach
Client:	Städtische Wohnbaugesellschaft Lörrach, Schillerstrasse 4, D-79540 Lörrach
Dates:	construction 1990–1994

STADION HOUSING DEVELOPMENT

Haagenerstrasse / Wintersbuckstrasse, D-79539 Lörrach | Bus 7: Heithemstrasse

Linear access and large balconies

The oval of a former sports arena is the site of a housing development by architects Wilhelm + Partner in Lörrach. The four-storey complex consists of fourteen buildings with a total of 220 residential units. Access is provided by a network of roads and paths intersecting at right angles. Archway buildings are located at the mid-point on each side while driveways provide access at the curved sections of the oval. The units in the buildings located at the two semi-circles have continuous front-to-back floor plans; in combination with the balconies to both courtyard and street front, this layout results in units that are flooded with light. The floor plans diminish into rounded triangles. The development is surrounded by rows of low-rise residential buildings, single and multi-family homes; from a planning perspective, the area seems rather rural. The new development has increased the density and thus the urban character of the area.

Aerial view of housing development

Architect:	Detlef Würkert and Hans Ueli Felchlin, Feldbergstrasse 1, D-79539 Lörrach
Client:	Städtische Wohnbaugesellschaft Lörrach, Schillerstrasse 4, D-79540 Lörrach
Dates:	project planning and construction 1994–1997

NANSENPARK HOUSING DEVELOPMENT

Nansenstrasse 5/7/Gretherstrasse/Haagenerstrasse, D-79539 Lörrach |

Bus 1 2 3 7 15 16: Gewerbeschule

Facade on Nansenstrasse

Entrance hall

North of the downtown, Detlef Würkert and Hans Ueli Felchlin have created two buildings with twenty-one residential units and four office or clinic spaces as well as a car park. The envelopes are in tune with the built environment of this former villa neighbourhood. The three-storey-high residential buildings extend into L-shapes created by two-storey office and clinic wings along the street front. Two fully glazed lobbies provide access to twenty-one apartments – three four-room units, twelve three-room units, and six two-room units – with large balconies above covered walkways. Two monumental wintergardens are the focal point of the structure.

Architect:	Wilfrid and Katharina Steib, Unterer Rheinweg 56, 4057 Basel
Client:	Stadt Lörrach, Stadtbauamt, Luisenstrasse 16, D-79537 Lörrach
Dates:	competition 1995, construction 1996–1998

AUF DEM BURGHOF THEATRE AND CONVENTION COMPLEX

Herrenstrasse 5, D-79539 Lörrach | Bus 3 6 7 16: Burghof | Train: Lörrach Bahnhof

The entrance portal

With the Burghof concert, theatre, convention, and exhibition complex Wilfrid and Katharina Steib have realized a multifunctional public building for the city of Lörrach. The 84-metre-long roof rises gently to the south where the theatre is located. The hall, with seating in a prototype design, has a maximum capacity of 900 visitors. Acoustics and ventilation are regulated by means of a specially designed wood floor and louvred mahogany panelling. Along the street front, the facade is nearly hermetically sealed, while a glass skin opens the building up on the courtyard side. The interiors in bold red and blue with shimmering ribbons of milk glass set into the flooring and the stairs create a tranquil and focused atmosphere.

L | LÖRRACH

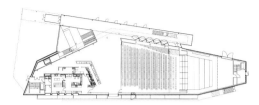

Ground floor

The large hall

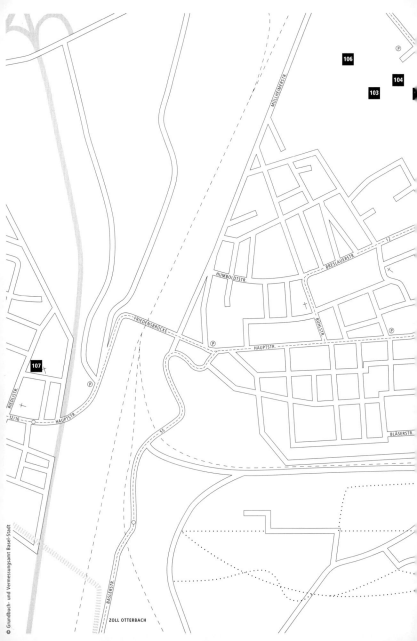

M | WEIL AM RHEIN

Architect:	Nicholas Grimshaw and Partners, Conway Street 1, London W1T 6 LR
Client:	Vitra GmbH, Charles-Eames-Strasse 2, D-79576 Weil am Rhein
Dates:	project planning and construction 1981

VITRA FURNITURE FACTORY

Charles-Eames-Strasse 2, D-79576 Weil am Rhein | Bus 12 55: Vitra

Detail of facade

When Nicholas Grimshaw rebuilt the burnt-down Vitra factory in just six months in 1981, the tight schedule was made possible by one particular circumstance: the building in Weil is one of many industrial buildings designed by the British architect. It resembles his design for a factory in Bath (1976) in many aspects: the cubature is almost identical, as are the access lanes and entrances, and the arrangements of the delivery and loading areas. The facades are clad in industrial materials and the corners rounded off. Grimshaw added six supply towers to the large structure (11 900 m^2) at rhythmic intervals. A prefabricated concrete frame with a 25-metre span is the key structural element.

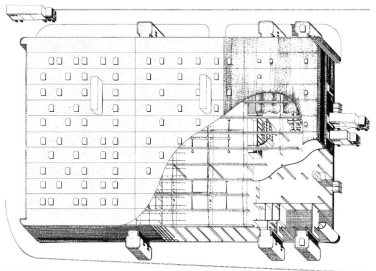

Axonometric

The north-east facade

Architect:	Frank O. Gehry + Associates, 1520B Cloverfield Boulevard,
	Santa Monica, California 90404 USA
	Project management, planning and supervision Günter Pfeifer,
	Industriestrasse 2, D-79541 Lörrach, in partnership with Roland Mayer
Client:	Vitra GmbH, Charles-Eames-Strasse 2, D-79576 Weil am Rhein
Dates:	project planning 1987, construction 1988–1989

VITRA DESIGN MUSEUM

Charles-Eames-Strasse 1, D-79576 Weil am Rhein | Bus 12 55: Vitra

The building with rectangular roof
above entrance area (right)

In his first European building – the Vitra Design Museum – Frank O. Gehry has created a floor space of 740 square metres. A cross-vault that seems to be inspired by the Gothic style provides interior support for a ceiling made to look ethereal with two large light wells. The upstairs is designed as a galleria and the walls merge in intersecting perspectives. Here, the design makes no attempt to guide the eye by means of sight-lines created by enfilades or vertical perspectives. The convex, foreshortened, and curved shapes of the dynamic building are best appreciated when standing in front of the entrance, where one also has an ideal view of the rectangular roof which seems to float above the entrance. From its inception the building has been compared to Le Corbusier's church at Ronchamp (1950–1954). Tadao Ando's conference pavilion is located next door (project 105).

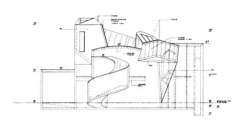

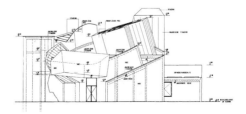

Elevations and sections of the animated building fabric

Architect:	Tadao Ando, 5–23, Toyosaki, 2-Chome Kita-ku, Osaka 531, Japan
	Project management, planning, site supervision Günter Pfeifer, Industriestrasse 2,
	D-79541 Lörrach, in partnership with Roland Mayer
Client:	Vitra GmbH, Charles-Eames-Strasse 2, D-79576 Weil am Rhein
Dates:	project 1989, construction 1992–1993

VITRA CONFERENCE PAVILION

Charles-Eames-Strasse 1, D-79576 Weil am Rhein | Bus 12 55: Vitra

Stairs to courtyard

A conference pavilion for the Vitra company was Japanese architect Tadao Ando's first European project in 1993. He created 420 square metres of floor space on two levels. The building surrounds a sunken courtyard, which gives the complex a monastic atmosphere. The property itself – and its cherry trees – contribute to the intimate quality of the architecture. The master builder realized yet another project based on his classic theme: the dialogue between "built" and "grown" architecture. The complex features unfinished concrete walls and American red oak flooring. The scheme accommodates one conference and three seminar rooms, a guest room, a library, and space for the building installations. The house lies directly next to Frank O. Gehry's Vitra Design Museum (project 104).

WEIL AM RHEIN

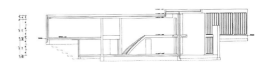

North-south section

The garden facade

Architect:	Alvaro Siza da Vieira, Rua do Aleixo, 53-2, 4150-043 Porto, Portugal
	Project management, planning, site supervision Günter Pfeifer,
	Industriestrasse 2, D-79541 Lörrach, in partnership with Roland Mayer
Client:	Vitra GmbH, Charles-Eames-Strasse 2, D-79576 Weil am Rhein
Dates:	project planning 1991, construction 1992–1993

VITRASHOP FACTORY HALL

Charles-Eames-Strasse 2, D-79576 Weil am Rhein | Bus 12 55: Vitra

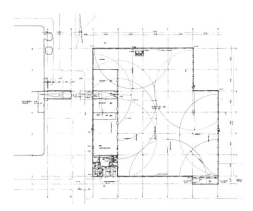

Ground floor

Alvaro Siza realized a single-storey factory hall for Vitra with a footprint of over 20 000 square metres. At 11 metres in height, the flat-roofed building is located next to the vast railway-yard of the Deutsche Bahn. With its clinker-brick facade, granite base, and rhythmically arranged 4-metre-high windows, the building resembles a minimalist sculpture. The vocabulary of this facade has much in common with the architectonic language of early industrial buildings. The gigantic hall has an interior ceiling height of 9 metres, where slender metal pylons create a simplicity and clarity of line usually associated with the naves of Romanesque churches. Tadao Ando's pavilion (project 105) and Siza's factory hall solidly anchor the company grounds and also provide a barrier to the north.

The factory seen from
Charles-Eames-Strasse

The monolithic building next to
Zaha M. Hadid's fire station

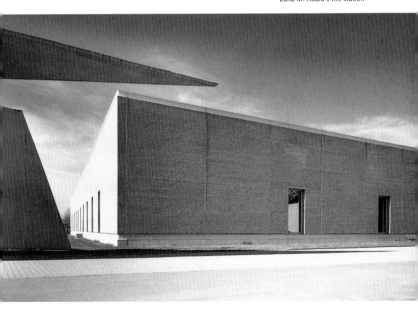

Architect:	Herzog & de Meuron, Rheinschanze 6, 4056 Basel
Client:	U. and R. Frei-Reimann, Fischingen
Dates:	project planning 1981, construction 1981–1982

FREI PHOTO STUDIO

Riedlistrasse 41, D-79576 Weil am Rhein | Bus 12 16: Riedlistrasse

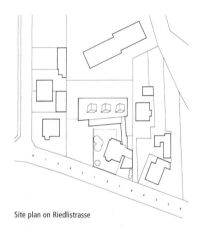

Site plan on Riedlistrasse

Herzog & de Meuron added a photo studio to a detached house in Weil. The new addition and a connecting corridor create a U-shaped complex on the 1900-square-metre property. The original building – a massive, two-storey stone house from the late nineteenth century with a square plan, a hipped roof, and an oriel – is now confronted by a trapezoid with a gently sloped shed roof and three cubed skylights that resemble great boulders. The facade clad in planks, plywood, and asphalt subscribes to an "aesthetic of poverty;" the cubed skylights, on the other hand, re-interpret the shed roof typology while adding a sculptural element.

Detail of facade in plywood

The studio with cubed skylights

Architect:	Zaha M. Hadid in collaboration with Schumacher, mayer bährle
	Zaha M. Hadid, Studio 9; 10, Bowling Green Lane, London EL1R OBD
	mayer bährle, Mühlestrasse 16, D-79539 Lörrach
Client:	Landesgartenschau Weil am Rhein 1999 GmbH,
	Mattrain 10, D-79576 Weil am Rhein
Dates:	project planning and construction 1996–1999

TRINATIONAL ENVIRONMENTAL CENTRE

Mattrain 1, D-79576 Weil am Rhein | Bus 55: Grün 99 | Train: Weil-Gartenstadt

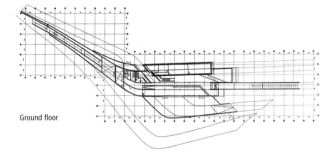

Ground floor

A pavilion designed by Zaha M. Hadid for the national garden show "Green 99" has been converted for use as an environmental centre. The 140-metre-long building is an urban anchor in the rural space between south Weil and Basel. A ramp-like path bisects the entire building along the middle axis, creating an inviting gesture to take a stroll. Expansive glazed sections infuse the expressive building with light and energy. The building is exclusively constructed from poured concrete, and the individualistic geometric treatment gives it a sculptural presence. The ground plan reveals similarities to basilica plans, similarities that are less evident on the interior. The main entrance, for example, opens onto a raised central aisle with a view of the left side aisle, while the right aisle lies hidden behind a dividing wall. The central aisle is topped by a ribbon of windows much like the clerestories in a church.

The ramp-like path onto the roof

ILLUSTRATION INDEX OF PROJECTS AND MAPS

Altenkirch, Dirk | 99↗ | 101↖↗
Arazebra, Helbing & Kupferschmid | 47←↗
Atelier Fontana | 32←→
Bensberg, Ralph | 42→
Biondo, Adriano | 71↘
Bisig, Tom | 5↗↘ | 43→↘
Blaser, Werner | 94↗
Bräuning, Niggi | 3→ | 63→ | 90↗↘ | 93
Bryant, Richard | 87↖ | 105←→
Clerc, HR + P | 18→
Disch Photograph | 49↗↘
Ege, Hans | 42→
Fotostudio M. Wolf | 55↗↘
Giese, André | 13↖→ | 15←→
Grimshaw, Nicholas & Partners | 103↗
Helbling, A. & Ineichen | 29↖ | 95↗↘
Helfenstein, Heinrich | 14↗↘ | 34←→
Herzog & de Meuron | 28← | 53←→ | 75→↘
Hessmann, Karin | 104←
Isler, Vera | 60↘
Jecklin, Cilla | 17←→ | 72↖
Kehl, Lilli | 26↖↗
Lichtenberg, Christian | 4↗↘ | 6↗↘ | 33↗
Meyer, Erich | 100→
Muelhaupt, André | 60↗
Musi, Pino | 48↗ | 57←↘
PlanetObserver.com | Satellite photo
Reid, Jo and Peck, John | 103←↘
Richters, Christian | 108→
Schweizerischer Bankverein | 70↖
Scherrer, Theodor | 45↘ | 61↗↘
Schulthess, Kathrin | 83←→

Spiluttini, Margherita | 8↗↘ | 9↗↘ | 11←→ | 23↗ | 27↘ | 28→ | 51↗↘ | 77←↘ | 80↗↘ | 107↗↘
Stutz, Ruedi | 98→
Voegelin, Andreas | 2← | 10↗↘ | 91↗↘
Walti Ruedi | 1→ | 6→↘ | 16←→ | 24→ | 31↘ | 35↘ | 37↗ | 41↗ | 45← | 50↖↗ | 53→ | 56←→ | 67→ | 68← | 75←↗ | 76↘ | 81← | 82↖ | 86→ | 88←→ | 92↖↗ | 102←→ | 106↗↘ |
Windhöfel, Lutz | 27↗ | 40←
Würkert, Detlef | 99↘
Zimmermann, Jürg | 77↗↘

Permission for reproduction of the maps 12 May 2004: Maps A, D, G, K, L, M: Grundbuch- und Vermessungsamt Basel-Stadt, Map I: Vermessungs- und Meliorationsamt Basel-Landschaft, Maps B, C, E, F, H, J: kant. Vermessungsämter BL und BS

Abbreviations: the arrows indicate the position of the photographs on each project double page.
Top right: ↗ bottom right: ↘ bottom left: ↙
top left: ↖ right: → left: ←

Unless otherwise indicated, the photographs and maps were created by the architects themselves or commissioned by each firm. We have made every effort to locate and list the copyright for all illustrations. Where the copyright is not listed, it is either held by the architect or we have been unable to determine the copyright holder, in which case we would ask the copyright holder to contact the publisher.

INDEX OF NAMES

The numbers set in black indicate buildings by these architects featured in the guide.

Ackermann & Friedli | 34 | 79
Alder, Michael | Introduction | 17 | 29 | 47 | 60 | 78 | 95
Alioth Langlotz Stalder Buol | Foreword | 20
Ando, Tadao | Introduction | 80 | 104 | 105 | 106
Artaria, Paul | 95
Baader, Stefan | 32
Barcelo Baumann Architekten | Foreword | 19
Baur, Hermann | 10 | 11 | 71
Bernoulli, Hans | 89 | 95
Berrel Architekten | Foreword | Introduction | 25 | 76
Beyeler, Ernst | Introduction | 93
Blaser, Werner | Introduction
Bo, Jørgen and Wohlert, Vilhelm | 93
Bonatz, Paul, Büchi, Paul and Christ, Rudolf | 59
Botta, Mario | Introduction | 48 | 57 | 58
Brüderlin, Rolf | 89
Brogli Esther & Müller, Daniel | 18
Brunner, R. and Dalla Favera, A. | 45
Bürgin & Nissen | Introduction | 52
Bürgin Nissen Wentzlaff | 58 | 86 | 88
Burckhardt Partner | Foreword | Introduction | 55 | 57 | 66 | 69 | 93
Buser, Bruno & Zaeslin, Jakob | 33
Buser, Renate | 24
Butscher, Christoph | 4
Calatrava, Santiago | Introduction
Callierotti, Alex and Pontillo, Giuseppe | 89
Cruz/Ortiz | Foreword | 67
Danuser, Hans | 68
Diener & Diener | Foreword | Introduction | 12 | 20 | 30 | 38 | 39 | 43 | 46 | 49 | 59 | 62 | 65 | 70
Dill, Christian | 45
Diserens, Eric | 27
Eames, Charles und Ray | Introduction

Eigenheer, Samuel | 18
Egli, Lukas | 35 | 37
Erny, Gramelsbacher, Schneider | 30
Fabro, Luciano | 59
Fahrni + Breitenfeld | 69
Fasnacht, François | 85 | 91
Fehlbaum, Rolf | Introduction
Felchlin, Hans Ueli and Würkert, Detlef | 99 | 101
Fierz Architekten | Foreword | 5
Fierz & Baader | 3 | 13 | 15
Fingerhuth, Carl | Introduction
Fürstenberger, Philippe | 51
Furrer, Rolf | 91
Gehry, Frank O. | Introduction | 87 | 104 | 105
Gigon, Annette | 23 | 80
Giraudi & Wettstein | Foreword | 67
Gmür, Silvia | Introduction | 4 | 74
Gmür, Silvia and Nussbaumer, Kurt, Suter+Suter, Toffel+ Berger | 10
Gmür/Vacchini | Foreword | 2 | 11
Gramelsbacher, Urs | Introduction | 16 | 61
Grasser, Thomas and Müller, Carmen | 84
Grimshaw, Nicholas | Introduction | 103
Gritsch, Hans and Segessenmann, Stephan | 71
Hadid, Zaha M. | Introduction | 108
Haller, Bruno and Fritz | 24
Herzog & de Meuron | Foreword | Introduction | 8 | 9 | 23 | 27 | 28 | 51 | 53 | 56 | 75 | 77 | 80 | 107
Hotz, Theo | 42
Huber, Dorothee | Introduction
Judd, Donald | 15 | 68
Kahn, Louis I. | 93
Karpf, Bernhard | 22
Kaufmann, Andreas and Tannenberger, Heiri | 14
Keller, Nadja | 82
Kempf, Marianne | 35
Kowanz, Brigitte | 68

INDEX OF NAMES

Krarup Furrer | Foreword | 76
Krischanitz, Adolf | Introduction
Kunz, Manfred | 41
Künzel, August | Foreword | 28 | 43 | 73
Lazzarini, Kurt | 56
Le Corbusier | Introduction | 104
Leisinger, Karl | 35
Levy, Renée | 77
Marbach, Ueli and Rüegg, Arthur | 7
Marques, Daniele | Foreword | 41
mayer bährle | 108
Mayer, Roland | 87 | 96 | 97 | 104 | 105 | 106
Meier, Mario | 8
Meier, Richard | Introduction | 22 | 70
**Metron AG (Markus Gasser,
Urs Deppler, Heini Glauser)** | 90
Mies van der Rohe, Ludwig | 41 | 84 | 93
Miller, Quintus & Maranta, Paola | Introduction | 31
Morellet, François | 68
Morger & Degelo | Foreword | Introduction | 1 | 35 | 37 | 41 | 81 | 82
Müller, Hanspeter | 17 | 29 | 72
Mumenthaler, Ursula | 68
Naef, Studer & Studer | Introduction | 6
Naegelin, Roland | 17 | 47 | 60 | 78 | 95
Nauman, Bruce | Introduction
Nyffeler, Stephan | 64
Offermann, Erich | 41
Panozzo, Giovanni | 71
Pfeifer, Günter | Introduction | 87 | 96 | 97 | 104 | 105 | 106
Piano, Renzo | Introduction | 93
Proplaning | 28 | 44 | 54 | 83
Rauch, Martin | 73
Rickenbacher, Fritz | 54
Rist, Pipilotti | 68
Roost, Andrea | Introduction | 14

Sacher, Paul | Introduction | 48
Salvisberg, Otto Rudolf | 59
Schaudt Architekten | 98
Scheiwiller & Oppliger | 50
Scheiwiller, Andreas | 84
Schmidt, Hans | 95
Schuldt, Klaus | 84
Schumacher, Patrick | 108
Schwarz, Rosmarie | 18
Schwarz, Guttmann, Pfister | Foreword | 64
Sieverding, Hans | 85
Siza da Vieira, Alvaro | Introduction | 106
Spycher, Ernst | Introduction
Stefani, Daniel & Wendling, Bernard | 26
Steib, Wilfrid and Katharina | Introduction | 21 | 33 | 36 | 40 | 63 | 94 | 102
Steidle, Otto | Introduction
Steiner, Georg | 48
Steiner, Rudolf | Introduction | 82
Stettler, Martin | 25
Stiner, Peter | Foreword | 73
Stump & Schibli Architekten | Foreword | 92
Suter & Burckhardt | 2
Tinner, Mathis S. | 9
Vadi, Tibère | 89
Van de Velde, Henry | 93
Varini, Felice | 57
Vischer Architekten | Introduction | 4
Weber, Adrian | 18
Wilhelm + Partner | 100
Wright, Frank Lloyd | 93
Würkert, Detlef | 99 | 101
Wymann & Selva | 71
Zinkernagel, Peter | 24
Zoderer, Beat | 68
Zürcher, Cornelia | 7
Zwimpfer Partner | Foreword | Introduction | 52 | 68 | 76

INDEX OF BUILDING TYPES AND USES

Buildings for children and youth | 26 | 72

Schools | 12 | 24 | 31 | 34 | 35 | 66 | 71 | 89

Training centres, meeting halls, and conference centres | 15 | 19 | 70 | 105 | 108

Research and university buildings | 4 | 5 | 6 | 9 | 13 | 14

Single-family houses | 25 | 74 | 77 | 78 | 80 | 82 | 84 | 96

Multi-family houses | 8 | 16 | 35 | 37 | 60 | 61 | 99 | 101

Residential buildings | 6 | 40 | 101

Residential developments | 29 | 30 | 33 | 38 | 39 | 44 | 49 | 83 | 90 | 95 | 100

Residential and office buildings (mixed use) | 7 | 23 | 43 | 49 | 56 | 62 | 65 | 69 | 85 | 86

Retail stores and shopping centres | 2 | 46 | 53 | 86

Office and administration buildings | 3 | 21 | 22 | 41 | 54 | 55 | 57 | 58 | 59 | 68 | 81 | 87 | 88 | 103

Industrial buildings and fair halls | 32 | 41 | 42 | 52 | 106 | 107

Transportation buildings | 51 | 67 | 91

Hotels and cafés | 19 | 41 | 43 | 86 | 98

Sports complexes | 27 | 47 | 50 | 53 | 73 | 76

Libraries | 4 | 97

Cinemas and theater | 64 | 98 | 102

Museum buildings | 1 | 13 | 48 | 63 | 75 | 93 | 104

Church buildings | 16

Hospital and care facilities | 9 | 10 | 11 | 17 | 28 | 45 | 92

Nursing homes and buildings for community living | 18 | 20 | 36 | 53 | 79 | 94

Conversion, renovation, heritage preservation | 1 | 3 | 4 | 5 | 10 | 13 | 49 | 54 | 97

The publisher and the author would like to thank
the Claire Sturzenegger-Jeanfavre Foundation for its
generous support in making this architecture guide
to the city of Basel possible.

This book is also available in a German language edition
(ISBN 3-7643-7087-4). The first edition is also available
in a French language edition (ISBN 3-7643-6286-3).

A CIP catalogue record for this book is available from
the Library of Congress, Washington D.C., USA.
Deutsche Bibliothek Cataloging-in-Publication Data

Bibliographic information by Die Deutsche Bibliothek.
Die Deutsche Bibliothek lists this publication in the
Deutsche Nationalbibliografie; detailed bibliographic data
is available in the internet at http://dnb.ddb.de.

This work is subject to copyright. All rights are reserved,
whether the whole or part of the material is concerned,
specifically the rights of translation, reprinting, re-use
of illustrations, recitation, broadcasting, reproduction on
microfilms or in other ways, and storage in data banks.
For any kind of use, permission of the copyright owner
must be obtained.

Translation from German into English by
Elizabeth Schwaiger, Toronto
Design: Muriel Comby, Basel
Drawings: Nicole Leiner, Basel
Printed in Germany

© 2004 Birkhäuser – Publishers for Architecture,
  P.O. Box 133, CH-4010 Basel, Switzerland

Printed on acid-free paper
produced from chlorine-free pulp. TCF ∞
ISBN 3-7643-7082-3

9 8 7 6 5 4 3 2 1